Punching and Kicking

Punching and Kicking

Leaving Canada's Toughest Neighbourhood

KATHY DOBSON

Véhicule Press

Published with the generous assistance of The Canada Council for the Arts and the Canada Book Fund of the Department of Canadian Heritage.

Funded by the Government of Canada
Financé par le gouvernement du Canada | Canadä

Cover and title design by David Drummond
Cover photo by Gabor Szilasi
Set in Minion and MrsEaves by Simon Garamond
Printed by Marquis Book Printing Inc.

Dépôt légal, Library and Archives Canada and the Bibliothèque national du Québec, third trimester 2018.

LIBRARY AND ARCHIVES CANADA CATALOGUING IN PUBLICATION

Dobson, Kathy, author
Punching and kicking : leaving Canada's toughest neighbourhood / Kathy Dobson.

Issued in print and electronic formats.
ISBN 978-1-55065-500-1 (softcover). – ISBN 978-1-55065-507-0 (EPUB)

1. Dobson, Kathy – Childhood and youth. 2. Pointe-Saint-Charles (Montréal, Québec) – Biography. 3. Poor families--Québec (Province) – Montréal – Biography. 4. Journalists – Canada – Biography. I. Title.

FC2947.26.D63A32 2018   971.4'28092   C2018-900716-8
C2018-900717-6

Published by Véhicule Press, Montréal, Québec, Canada
www.vehiculepress.com

Distribution in Canada by LitDistCo
www.litdistco.ca

Distributed in the U.S. by Independent Publishers Group
www.ipgbook.com

Printed in Canada on FSC® certified paper.

For Nora Jean Dobson, the real Ruth in my life, who has always insisted I tell my truth. And for always swallowing those fangs whenever she knew I was feeling particularly scared or vulnerable, I love you.

And for Jenny, whose arrival in this world brought so much hope and promise, I knew the rest of my journey would be worth it, no matter what.

ACKNOWLEDGEMENTS

When my dad took his final breath, he was at home, sitting up on the couch. My sister Patricia had almost lost her job as she practically moved into our parent's apartment, taking care of our dad with our other sisters around the clock. I admit it was unfair that I, who had flown in to Hamilton from Montreal at the last minute, got to hold our dad's right hand as Patricia held his left when he took his last breath. After diagnosing him with end-stage lung cancer, the doctors had given him three months. But, not surprisingly if you had known him, dad managed to stretch out his death sentence for almost ten full months. He fought until the last second, telling my sister Patricia he wanted to see a sunrise one last time, and refusing to die until she'd open the drapes next to the couch he had been camped out on for the last few days of his life.

At my dad's funeral, so many people showed up the funeral director had to move his body to the larger viewing room. The minister who gave the eulogy kept making small mistakes. Dad had gotten religious in the last few months of his life, so he was new to the church and the minister was trying to pretend that he actually knew him. After he made a particularly dumb mistake, like calling my dad by the wrong name, I couldn't help myself, I snorted. I hadn't meant to, really I hadn't. I was mortified. But a second later, one of my sisters giggled softly and that was it. Now all six of us girls were laughing and crying so hysterically in the front pew, the rest of the room seemed frozen in horror. I was afraid to look at our mother, though I could feel her angry glare and fuming embarrassment directed at the back of my head.

If it's possible to have a perfect moment at a funeral, that would have been it. Throughout our lives, our dad had been the master of trying to make us laugh at the worst possible moments. And if there had been a worst possible moment in any of his children's lives, his funeral that day would have been it.

I think laughter, at the best and worst moments, is what makes almost anything bearable and if there's one thing my sisters and I share, it's the ability to laugh even during the darkest moments. For that, I thank our dad, who taught us that no matter how dark life gets, laughter is that little light that can brighten up even the darkest and scariest shadows.

This book, as with the first, would not have been possible without the endless support and encouragement from my two oldest children, Jenny and Scott. They not only acted as first readers and editors, they always told me the truth, no matter how annoyed they knew I might get.

Thanks also to my three other children, David, Michael and Sam, whose love, like laughter, proves that no matter how dark a day may seem, there's always something great waiting just around the corner.

And a very special thanks to my fearless publisher, Simon Dardick, who always knew to parcel out his edits very gently, and over time. You have always been right about everything, damn it. I deeply appreciate your wise advice, generous support, and patient guidance.

Chapter One

OKAY, I ADMIT IT. I can hold a grudge. Some say it's the curse of the Irish but my dad says it's a gift. I mean, don't get me wrong, I'm good at faking like I'm over it even when I'm not, especially once a person says they're sorry and owns their shit. Everybody makes mistakes, right? But fuck with me, or one of my sisters, big or small, and I'll be plotting until the day I get to give it right back to you. I admit to even enjoying the whole plotting revenge thing. Here's where I think most people get it wrong. They decide how to punish someone who has fucked with them by what they think is the worst thing that could happen to them. Which means, for example, that rich people think about suing. Piss them off and they're taking you to court, trying to take some of your money. Yeah, losing their money, that's their worst nightmare. But me? I try to figure out what's the worst thing that could happen to you, according to you. And then help make that happen. Yeah. I know, I know. It's not very nice. But fuck being nice with someone who has shit on you, right? And seriously, what's the point of revenge if it doesn't hit the mark? Of course, you gotta pick the right time to make your move since it's like what my best friend Jenny said one time about never letting the dragon know it's a dragon until you slay them.

My nanny isn't always the clearest speaker on the planet, if you know what I mean. But she's smart, real smart, and everyone who knows her knows that.

"Revenge is mine, sayeth the Lord," says Nanny.

See what I mean?

But... uh... about this whole revenge thing with God? Does that mean the rest of us have to always turn the other cheek? Let the shitheads smack us twice? Nanny is always saying it's not nice to hold so much anger and hate in my heart and that the Lord wants me to leave it in His hands to figure out how to deal with those who trespass against me. Or

11

something like that. I want to tell her that I have no problem with anyone who does a trespass, especially since I'm not even really all that sure what exactly it means anyway, though Ruth told me it means someone is sneaking around on my land, taking shortcuts and stuff without my permission. To be honest, if I ever own land one day I'll be okay with people walking around in my back or front yard, cutting through to maybe avoid the laneways and stuff. I sure as hell wouldn't be mean or crabby like the old biddy on Rozel Street who takes a shit fit if you even take some of the snow off her front step to make a snowball. You can imagine what happened the first time she told me to "give that back right now, it's mine!" But even when it comes to forgiveness, I'm more like my dad and Uncle Patrick than the Lord, thank god. I like everyone until I don't. Fuck with me or mine and I'll fuck with you and yours all day.

Dad waited seven years to get revenge on one guy. He was 11 years old when this twentysomething-year-old beat the crap out of him for giving him a "funny" look when he passed by. This was down in Gaspé when Dad was just a kid, after his dad had died and his older brother, Uncle Patrick, was overseas in the war. That guy knew Dad was alone in the world, except for his mother. Mind you, had Dad told Nanny what that guy had done to him outside of Warren's Tavern she would have taken him down on her own. But Dad never told her, of course. He never told anyone. Then his brother came back on leave and someone at the Tavern told him about seeing his little brother taking a beating like a man. When Uncle Patrick asked Dad what had happened, Dad looked him right in the face and swore on their father's memory and their mother's life that nothing had happened—nobody had laid a finger on him. My dad didn't want his older brother to get his revenge for him. He wanted to wait until he was bigger, and then he could get it himself.

Years later, Dad would learn that Uncle Patrick had paid a visit to the guy. He would insist he wasn't doing any form of payback. He understood that was up to Dad. He just wanted to know the truth of what had happened and, hey, if that took breaking every finger on both hands, snapping his collarbone when he pressed on it with the bottom part of a bar stool, and grinding his face into the pile of glass dust created from smashing the guy's heavy pint glass onto the bar, at least he learned the truth. Uncle Patrick wasn't as patient as Dad.

When Uncle Patrick was satisfied he had the whole story, once the guy stopped crying, he leaned in close and warned him about how much he'd enjoy looking him up if he ever got word, from *anyone*, about what had just gone down between them.

"My brother will come for you in a few years, and when he does, you want to look surprised. Once he's done with you, we're good. You won't ever see me again."

As Uncle Patrick expected, the guy left town before morning.

"I figured it might be better if Russell didn't have to face that piece of shit every time he walked by him before he was ready. And by then, that asshole would have convinced himself he's not afraid of me, and would move back to town just in time. My little brother would be all grown up."

Uncle Patrick is always saying cool stuff like that, explaining shit I didn't even know I needed to know until he tells me about it. I can see why my dad thinks he's the best brother in the world. He's the best uncle, too. Nanny says it's the gift of the Irish. They always have each other's back.

But my sister Annie isn't as big on revenge.

"You are only as good as the weakest person you try to help," says Annie. "Or something stupid like that," she added, and then we both laughed. I don't see revenge as helping or hurting weak people, though. Revenge makes me feel stronger. Or at least thinking about it does. It reminds me I won't always be smaller or weaker.

But Annie has read that lame quote about being weak and helping others off of one of those big stupid "inspirational" signs in the metro. I think she must have lost something in the translation, though. Or maybe that shit sounds more deep in French? My school has the same kind of dumb posters all over the hallways now and in the guidance counsellor's office. "Shoot for the moon. Even if you miss, you'll land among the stars." And "Victory Requires Payment in Advance." Seriously? Do they think some kid walking down the hallway or sitting in the guidance office sees that poster and stops dead in their tracks, reads it, and then... what?

Come on. Have you ever in your entire life read one sentence anywhere that changed what you think? Changed what you do? Annie always likes that kind of crap, though. She says it actually does make her stop and think.

Annie's the second oldest, after our sister Ruth, but we mostly considered Annie the oldest since Ruth lived with Nanny most of the time when she was growing up. I'm next and then there's Julia, Beth, and then the youngest, Hanna. Our mom had us one after another with a short break between me and Julia for our brother, the one that didn't make it past seven months. Mom always says us kids are why she didn't get to see her toes for seven years. I still roll my eyes just thinking about her saying that, but to be fair, Mom has said and done even worse stuff than that. Thanks to making her fight with the welfare office practically a full-time job it seemed like it was rare when a week went by that she wasn't either on the six o'clock news facing off against the riot squad or marching around in front of the mayor's home in Westmount, or being interviewed in the Montreal *Gazette* about slum landlords in our neighbourhood. People are forever saying how smart she is and brave, but I don't know. Where has all of that yelling with the bullhorns and lesbians from McGill's School of Social Work got her, anyway? I'm pretty sure that's the reason why Dad stays away most of the time, too. Annie says it's because of the social workers being able to just show up anytime they want and be able to search our place and make sure Dad or any other men aren't hanging around. I'm not sure I believe that. I mean, it doesn't make any sense, right? Why would a social worker want to punish Mom for letting Dad come over, anyway?

"Mom would lose her welfare cheque," says Annie, "and then we'd all be in big trouble."

"Why would they take away Mom's welfare cheque just 'cause of Dad being here?"

"I'm not sure," admits Annie, "but if you have a man around, you aren't allowed any money."

That's just stupid. Maybe social workers are all lesbians, just like Dad always says, and that's why they don't like men? Dad says they're all angry dykes and when I asked Ruth later what an angry dyke is she said that's a woman who is mad at all the men in the world and likes to kiss a girl's peach parts. I'm pretty sure she's messing with me, though, hoping I'll ask Mom if it's true and then have Mom tell me I'm an idiot again. Ever since Mom found out when I was little that I was pretty sure that Ruth is a vampire she doesn't believe anything I say anymore. But I think the social worker shows up so she can act like the boss. I hate it when she knocks on the door and if we don't answer it within a couple of seconds, will actually yell through the door.

"I KNOW YOU'RE HOME. OPEN THE DOOR. NOW. PLEASE."

Like saying "please" makes it okay to yell and let the whole damn block know our social worker has arrived for a surprise home visit. And why do they call it a "home visit," by the way? I thought a "visit" was something friends and family do. And if friends or family strolled around like they owned the place, making tsk-ing sounds as they roamed from room to room, even taking a peek in the bathroom, you'd kick them out on their ass. I heard Mom telling Aunt Edna one time that it's an invasion and should be called an "occupation by the goddamn welfare office." But Mom always knows to keep her cool and not let the social worker get her going. She pretends not to be embarrassed, though I know she's dying inside because of the messy kitchen table and all of the stuff lying around. Mom always says it's impossible to keep stuff clean with six kids all under the age of 12.

"Between that and the roaches, what does the city really expect me to do?"

It's the roaches that will usually get the social worker outta there pretty fast. Mom always offers the worker a cup of coffee she knows she doesn't have, but also knows they'll never take. It would mean drinking it out of one of our cups. And Lord knows, Mom always says, how many roaches might have been doing the cha-cha in the bottom of the cups, just waiting for a kettle of boiling water to send them all to hell. I think she's being funny, though. Roaches don't like boiling water and I've never seen any of them doing the cha-cha, or any other dance. If anything, they just run when you get too close, scattering like a nest of mice suddenly disturbed, all rushing off in different directions.

"Now, who sleeps in here?" asks the social worker. She's looking at me. We have three bunk-bed sets in the room she's pointing at with her head. I look at Mom. I'm not sure if I'm supposed to pretend to be simple in the head or deaf. Mom and Dad have told us girls about a million times never to answer any social worker's questions about nothing. Or teachers. Or bill collectors. Or the Jew. Or the cops. Or nosy neighbours.

"I'm talking to you," says the social worker. I know I'm not allowed to bark back at her to fuck off, even if I'd be willing at that moment to give up my turn for wearing socks tomorrow just to be able to see the look on her face if I did. Before I have to decide, though, Mom answers her for me.

"Oh, she's a shy one," says Mom. Her smile doesn't reach her eyes but the social worker doesn't seem to notice. Or care.

"All of my kids sleep in there," says Mom. "They each have their own bed and blankets. If you look, you'll see I have..."

"What's your name?" asks the social worker. Now she's the one playing deaf, like she didn't hear a word Mom just said.

"What?" I know how to fuck with this bitch all day.

"I asked you what your name is," said the social worker. Her face is getting smaller and tighter by the moment.

"Uh? Come again?"

"Your name. What is your name?"

"She's Kathy," says Mom. "Her name is Kathy. She's almost ten."

The worker looks at Mom now. "Is she a special-needs child?" She looks down at her file folder, looking through her papers, trying to find the notes, the ones that say my mom has a retard.

"Huh?" I can't help myself. I know Mom is gonna kill me later. But I can't help myself.

"Uh, no, she's fine," says Mom. "She's just a little, you know, she's a little... shy. Really."

The worker suddenly drops her pile of stuff and screams. It's like she's wrapped in an invisible fire and she's burning up. She's whacking at her own body like she needs to put the fire out. Her papers are all over the floor and even her fancy small suitcase is lying at her feet. Mom rushes over to help. I try not to bust a gut on the spot. I'm already writing the story in my head for Annie later, even before I know how this one ends.

"Here! Here!" says Mom, trying to hand some of the stuff off the floor back to the worker.

"Noooooo," says the worker, stepping back and waving her hands like Mom is trying to hand her a small pile of steaming dog shit or something. That's when I saw the roach. She had knocked it off and didn't see it near her right foot yet. Sometimes the tiny fuckers will play dead and freeze. Like a game of Mother May I? Only this guy was still waiting for further instructions. Without thinking, I rushed over and crushed the fucker underneath my shoe. The loud crunching sound made the social worker jump. I grinned at her, letting her know I understood how gross it is. I'm not sure she got it, though, as she instantly got all up in our faces again.

"Obviously someone needs to stay on top of the mess in this apartment!" she said, making it clear who that "someone" is when she glared at my mother like she had sent out a pet roach in attack mode, just to hear her scream half the damn block down.

"I'm sorry!" said Mom, "I do everything I can to stay on top of them but the landlord ignores me and when I spray too much it makes the kids all cough and the youngest just throws everything up…"

I hate watching Mom like that. I like it better when she's Mad Mom, ranting and swearing and threatening to "expose" the city and welfare office.

The worker is giving each piece of her papers off the floor a small shake before shoving it back into her tiny suitcase. She looks under each piece like she expects to see something hiding there as she turns it over. I'm glad when she finally leaves in a breathless huff a few minutes later. But I wonder why finding a man in our place would have still been worse than finding a cockroach? I mean, Dad is a good guy. But Mom is crying now. She closed the bathroom door but I can still hear her. She's saying she hates the fucking Point and please god, please let her move. Please help her escape. Please help her save her children.

I'm glad she wants to save me. I thought she would kill me after the worker left. I wonder what Mom wants to save us from exactly? The fleas and bedbugs? Sure, they can be a pain in the ass but they aren't scary, just

17

gross. Sometimes when we're about to watch some cartoons on Saturday morning while Mom is still sleep, one of us will yell, "I forgot my water!" then rush off to the kitchen to get their glass so they can drop the fleas or bedbugs picked off an elbow or knee into the water. By the end of the *Bugs Bunny Show* or *Batman* episode there can be three layers of bugs. The top layer still squirming like a furry rug, the ones that didn't drown still trying to use the bodies of the ones beneath like a raft, then the ones that have sunk to the bottom. We nearly always remember to dump the glasses outside in the lane and put the glass back in the kitchen before Mom even wakes up. But the roaches? I mean, I heard roaches are practically everywhere, and rats are, too. Maybe landlords are better where rich people live, though? Maybe they spray more often and have really heavy toilet lids, so the rats can't climb up the pipes and bump their heads against the lids until they pop right out?

"Rich people don't have to let social workers in when they just show up like that," says Annie. "Rich people know their rights. They aren't afraid to tell the bitch to come back later at a more convenient time."

That makes me and Annie laugh for a bit. Her using a fancy word like "convenient." We heard the social worker say that word one time and it took us a minute to realize she was talking about the corner store. Most of us call it a *dépanneur,* or dép, of course. Even the English call it that in Montreal. But social workers call it a "convenience store." God, they're so dumb, right?

Mom always says one day she's going to take us out of the Point. Dad says it, too. One day we're going to move to Ville LaSalle, where Nanny says everyone has jobs and no one beats their wives or has filthy roaches or rats. My cousin Bruce says that's a lie.

"Half the dads in LaSalle beat the shit out of their women, too."

It must be nice not to have roaches and rats, and everybody having jobs, though, right?

"It's expensive, though," explains Bruce. "The rents are like fucking crazy. And they make you pay a first month's rent and what would be your last month's rent, even before they'll let you park one box or garbage bag in the place."

How can you know what will be your last month there, though, I wonder? We move all the time, every three months or so, all over the Point. And seriously, if you had two months' rent in your pocket, wouldn't you just buy the place? Annie says she'd stay in the Point and just buy all kinds of cool stuff for everybody.

"I'd buy one of those huge tins of cleaning stuff like the one they use at the school and a whole bunch of real toilet paper, the kind they sell at the store. I'd also find out where the landlord buys his roach killer and buy enough for our whole street. Nanny says if you leave even one alive anywhere nearby it will move in and send out a signal to all of its friends and family to come and join them and take over in a couple of days. We need to do our whole street!"

Annie says she'd also buy us girls all our own set of socks and underwear. And if she had anything left over, she'd buy all of us some new winter boots and get rid of those old bread bags we always use to stop the wet coming in through the holes in our boots.

"We'd have dry feet at school all day!" says Annie. "No more wet and funny smelling feet each night."

I like it when Annie talks about the stuff she'd fix. It makes us both laugh and think hard and rearrange our choices and picks over and over again until we know we've got it just right. I always say that first I'd move far away from the Point. I'd move to that place on TV that has moms who wear aprons and make cookies just because, and where the dads get to live with their kids all the time and don't just visit sometimes and social workers can't take away your mom's welfare cheque just because she catches your dad shivering in the cold on the balcony, hoping she won't think to look out there. I'd live in that place where moms don't say "Fuck!" and dads don't say "Sssh, it's okay. It's okay," while nothing is really okay. Yeah, I'd use my money to move to that place.

"That place doesn't exist on earth," says Annie. "That's why you gotta just fix what you have instead of trying to find something that just isn't out there."

"Oh, great, you get to say you wanna live in a world where roaches are too afraid to come to your block 'cause they'll get gassed, and everyone has their own socks and underwear to wear every single day and never has to borrow or share, and that's real and okay. But I want to move to that place where social workers are not the boss of me and *I'm* the crazy one."

I like laughing with Annie. When I'm with her I know for sure, no question, anything can happen. She always says if you can think of it, then it can happen. You just have to think of it. I'm always trying to think up the best stuff ever when I'm with Annie.

"What about a place where uncles don't hurt kids?" I ask, then instantly regret it. This game is supposed to be fun. Now I've ruined it.

"Well," says Annie slowly, "...maybe in the new place we could have a rule about no uncles allowed?" But she quickly changes her mind. She remembers Uncle Patrick, Dad's big brother, is good. He'd never hurt any of us girls. I want to say that in the new place we could just have a rule about being allowed to say what's really going on and not have to worry about Dad going to jail because he'd get so angry he'd kill anyone who ever lay a hand on any of us girls, or Mom having to maybe stop talking to her own brothers ever again. But I know Annie will just feel sad so I laugh and then ask her what food we'd eat in this new place.

"I'd have fried eggs!" says Annie. "And not just the crunchy leftover parts. I'd have the whole thing, even the yellow middle part!"

She likes this game. A lot.

"And I'd have toast with it, and jam on the toast. And some tea! And only real milk with the tea, too."

I don't have to think about it.

"I'd have real hot-dog buns with my hot dogs," I say.

None of that slice of bread wrapped and rolled around the wiener. Nope. A real hot-dog bun. No big white blanket around my dog, no way.

"Now you're being all fancy!" laughs Annie.

When our Aunt Colleen won a thousand dollars on a scratch ticket she was thrilled. She got to play out one of her biggest dreams, one she'd constantly talked about wanting to do if she ever got her hands on some serious bucks. She hired a whole bunch of people from the Point to play extra cards for her at Bingo. She'd been playing at the church Bingo for years and rarely won anything. Now with over two hundred cards in play she figured she'd found a foolproof way to win. After a month, though, with one of her Bingo slaves usually winning at least a small prize, everyone else in the hall was hating on her so much she decided maybe her dream wasn't all she had hoped it would be. Instead of owning the room like she thought she would, no one would talk to her anymore and no one cheered when one of her slaves would yell out, "BINGO!" She finally decided it wasn't worth it anymore.

"People are just such fucking poor losers and jealous, they took all the fun out of winning," she said. Her thousand dollars is now long gone, so she quit going to Bingo. Some claimed it was on account of her showing off and going broke, but others swore she was just going to the church Bingo in Verdun now.

As much fun as we have, I've decided not to tell Annie that Mom caught me writing on the wall in our room with chalk again. I'm afraid she'll laugh at me, though Annie never laughs in a mean way. At first Mom started to say something and then saw the chalk was white, same as the wall I was writing on. I'm not stupid. I wouldn't write on a coloured wall with white chalk. I was glad she didn't ask me where I got the chalk.

"What are you doing?" she asked.

Her voice had made me jump, even though she didn't sound mad or anything.

"Nothing." I said. "Just playing school."

I knew she'd believe that. All of my sisters' dolls and stuffed animals, even the busted and dirty ones, were sitting in front of me, just a few feet away in two messy but crowded rows. They looked like they were paying attention. Like they actually loved school and learning stuff.

"Oh," she said, then smiled and left the room.

I knew not to tell her the dolls and stuffies were, as Nanny would say, bearing witness. Not that they could read or hear, of course. I'm nearly ten so I know toys can't read or hear, even though I keep telling my baby sister Hanna that they can. Hanna can't read or write all that well yet cause she's only four so we taught her to just whisper her bad stuff into an empty box or shoe, or if she can't find anything else, just into her hands. Like we did when we were little like her. Hanna is always laughing and still bangs and smacks her hands on the highchair whenever she wants one of us to let her out. We usually all rush and try to be the one to get there first because whoever lifts that tray thing over her head gets a huge grin and a wet kiss. Hanna keeps saying she's a big girl now and wants to sit in a real chair like the rest of us kids but since we only have five chairs around the kitchen table, she's usually the one stuck in the highchair. Sometimes Beth is willing to change seats with her when she's in the mood to pretend to be a baby and make us all laugh while she says ga-ga and ma-ma and bangs her spoon on the tray. Beth is 11 months older than Hanna but she's still small enough to fit perfectly in the highchair. She gets all mad, though, if you try to say she's a baby, too, and likes to remind Hanna who the real baby in the family is.

"Me not a baby!" says Beth. "Hanna the baby!"

That usually makes Hanna start to yell that she's no baby, either, and then the two of them will start pointing at each other and screaming, "YOU THE BABY!"

I think Beth just hates being small and wants to make sure we don't forget she's getting bigger all the time now. As soon as one of them takes a breath during their screaming matches, the other will instantly yell, "Me NOT a baby!" and then whichever one is trapped in the highchair will try to get out so they can rush the other one. Seeing two babies go at it like that is pretty funny. One time, Hanna almost fell out of the chair, though, she was so frantic to get to Beth. Thank god, without even thinking, Beth instantly leaned over and grabbed her arm just before they both went crashing to the floor. Annie says Beth's quick reaction broke Hanna's fall, which is why she didn't get seriously hurt. But then the two of them started rolling around on the floor and smacking at each other, like two cats in a serious brawl that get so attached, you don't even know what part to grab onto to break it up. It took a minute for us all to stop laughing and figure out what to pull on just to get the two little jerks apart. We laughed about it later for days and days, telling Beth we were going to call her the toughest baby in the world from now on. That would usually piss Hanna off as she'd yell, "ME the toughest baby in the world!"

Beth really is pretty tough, even though she's tiny and skinny for a five-year-old. The only thing that seriously scares Beth, though, are clowns. The first time she really freaked out over one was last Christmas, when instead of getting a doll like my two older sisters Ruth and Annie, I got a stuffed clown. I mean, not that I didn't hate it on sight, too. But I wasn't afraid of it or anything, just disappointed. It had a white silk hat glued to the top of its head and a huge ugly red nose. The colours were different stripes up and down its pant legs and it wasn't even a girl clown. Ruth and Annie had twin dolls, both exactly the same with soft blonde hair that was going to need regular brushing to keep it beautiful, and light blue dresses and a white ribbon around the hems. These dolls looked like little rich girls. They were perfect. My ugly clown had plastic orange hair and weird shoes that didn't come off. He was too tall and not at all cuddly. I knew if I didn't pretend to love him my mom would be sad, though, and when she asked me all happily what I was going to name my clown, I knew not to say, "Fucking Ugly Head." Even though I didn't like my clown, I know Mom still paid something for him from the church bazaar.

"They only had two dolls at the sale," said Mom, "so I snatched them up for your sisters, of course. And when I saw the clown I instantly thought of you!"

Why would an ugly clown make my mom think instantly of me? My eyes hurt from trying to make them stay dry.

"Frankie," I suddenly said. "My clown's name is Frankie."

My two older sisters instantly lowered their eyes and got busy fussing with their new dolls. Julia was busy making horsey noises with her new stuffed purple pony, so I don't think she had heard me. Beth and Hanna were fighting over a green dinosaur; one of them saying it was a dog, the other insisting it was a fat rat.

"Well, that's an interesting choice," said Mom. "Frankie?"

"Yes, doesn't he look like a Frankie?" I said, holding him out in front of me.

"Look at me, I get to live with little girls now full-time," I said, making "Frankie's" voice as deep as I could.

At that moment Beth looked over. Maybe it was Frankie's voice, or maybe she really hadn't noticed my clown yet, but she stood up, dropping her green dog, and just opened her mouth and started to scream. No warning so we could brace our ears for the shock wave of her cries, just an unexpected sound wave rushing over the room and making everyone freeze in shock. Mom finally broke free of the wave and rushed towards her.

"Beth? What is it? What's wrong? Why are you yelling?" Mom was frantically doing a full-body check on Beth as she grilled her, searching for any threads wrapped tightly around a baby finger or a rat hiding in her pyjama bottoms, maybe gnawing on her small leg. Mom had told me one time that when a little one is crying for no obvious reason you have to quickly check and make sure they haven't somehow wrapped a teeny thread from their own clothing around a baby finger or toe, as they could actually cut it off by mistake. Ever since then, any time Hanna has started to cry for any reason, I always check her chubby little hands, followed by her teeny little feet. All checked. All clear. Then I'll ask her what's wrong. I figure there's no time to waste when it comes to toes and fingers maybe being cut off, right? And since one time Mom found one of my sisters looking like she was having a fit 'cause she was just standing there and screaming while her whole body trembled, her arms sticking out from her sides like a kid-sized scarecrow, but it turned out a mouse had just run up the sleeve of her shirt, Mom has learned to suspect mice or rats as potential invaders as well.

But as Mom did the full-body check on Beth, searching and pulling on her, and yelling at her face, "WHAT? WHAT? WHAT IS IT?" I wondered how she didn't get it. It was Frankie. The clown. Beth was afraid of my clown.

"It's Frankie!" I said, but at first no one could hear me. What with Mom yelling and Beth screaming, and now Hanna also wailing away, I had to shove Frankie into one of the boxes on the floor before Beth stopped to take a breath. A huge breath.

"It's Frankie!" I tried again. "Beth doesn't like him!"

Ruth tossed me a strange look, and then rushed over to Beth.

"Here, here," she said, holding out her new doll to Beth. "Why don't you hold 'Louise'? She'd love for you to hold her." Ruth smiled at Beth and gently placed one of Beth's small hands on Louise's hair. "See? She's so nice, right?"

I later made Annie laugh when I said, "Jesus Christ. So that's how you get a doll around this place?"

I already knew that Beth doesn't like clowns much. I mean, the good thing is that it's not like we're running into clowns left and right, anyway. But if she sees one in a picture book or on a cartoon she gets all quiet and sometimes even softly cries a little. It's the one thing we know not to bug her about. Clowns are off the table when it came to trying to mess with Beth. We all know that. Well, except for Mom, of course. But she's busy and not always paying real close attention, and to be fair, I hadn't thought about Beth when I first saw my clown, either. I was too busy being pissed off about getting stuck with someone's old lumpy toy from the church. Frankie even smells funny. But being afraid of a clown? To me clowns are kind of cool. In every story I've ever read with a clown in it they're the ones who are allowed to say truths that others are afraid to say and since they say it like they're joking, they can get away with it, right? Even kings used to let a clown mock them right to their face and say stuff someone else might get their head chopped off for. Maybe that's why Mom gave me a clown for Christmas. She knows I think they're kind of cool? But the Joker from *Batman* is a clown too, right? So maybe that's what started Beth off. Later, once all the excitement died down and Ruth and Annie had promised Beth she could take turns with helping them to care for their new dolls, Mom pulls me aside and says she hadn't forgotten I have a birthday coming up soon.

"And maybe you'll get a doll, too," she says with a smile. I smile back, knowing it wouldn't be a good idea to tell her I'd just decided on the spot that I hate dolls now. All of them. Even the pretty soft ones with silk ribbons and hair you can comb. Dumb shitheads. If she gives me a doll for my birthday I'm going to scribble all over its face, put it on fire and then drop it in the hole in Grandpa's kitchen floor.

I remember whispering my bad secrets into a broken doll's head when I was little. Mom saw me one time and thought I was talking to my doll, like I was an idiot who thought a doll with a broken head could hear me.

"I hate Uncle Frankie."

And Uncle Luther, too.

I did a lot of whispering into empty shoes and boxes when I was a little kid.

Chapter Two

"THE IRISH HAVE ALWAYS been solid storytellers," says Nanny. "They know how to tell a tall tale."

"The Irish are full of shit," says Mom, but her dad is from England so Nanny says it's to be expected that she'd be bitter about how great we are at telling stories. And keeping secrets. Mom keeps saying us kids aren't pure Irish, but I say we got all the best parts. Especially when it comes to telling stories. They say you should begin a story at the beginning, I say fuck that. Begin at the interesting part.

One time when my dad came home from the Legion, just before he fell asleep at the kitchen table, under his breath he softly said, "I killed all the wrong people."

How's that for starting with the good part?

But I knew I couldn't shake him awake, even after that, to ask him about it. Dad went to Korea when he was 17, during the war, so I've heard a lot of the stories but still, I wonder when or who he's talking about. Wrong people, from back in Korea? Or back when he was a cop? I know he wasn't a cop for all that long anyway, what with his brother borrowing his gun without even asking and Dad having to argue and beg him for weeks and weeks just to get it back before anyone would notice that if there were suddenly any bad guys who needed shooting, the bullets wouldn't be coming from Dad's missing gun. Maybe this is why he does what he does now, "taking care" of bad people. Making up for all those other bad people he didn't get when he was a cop for a while. Or maybe he actually means when he's working those jobs I sometimes get to sneak in and watch. Or maybe I didn't hear him right. Everybody always says I'm a troublemaker and a liar, so maybe I'm even making this up to myself. Dad says I always ask too many questions, too, and always at the wrong time. But Dad always says that, no matter when or where I ask the questions. He says I should be a reporter when I grow up since I like asking so many questions.

I wonder how someone becomes a reporter. I've seen reporters on TV during the six o'clock news talking to Mom or one of her gang at one of their sit-ins or street demonstrations outside the welfare office, or the mayor's mansion in Westmount. I've also watched them up close as they asked her a whole bunch of questions, a small notebook in their hand, as they seem to try and write down every single word she says. Sometimes Mom will suddenly catch herself and slow down.

"You have to make sure they get the best parts just right," explained Mom. "You don't want them to miss the gold."

But I think you have to be a good writer to be a reporter, and a fast writer, too. I mean, they stand there writing down every word someone says. That's gotta be tough, right? My mom talks pretty fast when she's mad or upset and sometimes even I don't know what the hell she's just said if she's super pissed. I've seen reporters trying to hide their shock sometimes at something Mom has said. You see the pen hover over the paper, and they always give it away by asking her to repeat it. Like they can't believe anyone would say something like that.

"I mean every word," says Mom. "The mayor needs to go fuck himself but first he needs to try living on seven bucks a week with six children, no man, and winter coming. My kids don't have coats, boots, hats or gloves for that kind of weather. What's the bastard going to do about it?"

Mom says you can always feel free to swear as much as you want to reporters, as they'd never dare to put that shit into the newspaper.

"But it sure makes them pay close attention while they're interviewing you," says Mom. "They like you to be colourful."

Dad says Mom has become an expert at manipulating the press now.

"Just don't start believing any of your own bullshit," says Dad.

To be a good reporter I guess you have to know people, too. Not just be a fast writer but also be able to read people, know when they're bullshitting you. And when they're telling the truth. My mom has always had a flexible friendship with the truth. She knows that sometimes you have to lie to tell the truth and has always taught us girls that the best truths are the versions that sound the most true. If nobody is gonna believe you but yourself, what's the point, right? So yeah, Mom says that sometimes you have to make up the truth so people will listen.

I wonder what happens when a reporter starts to interview someone and realizes they're boring? Do they ever say, "Oh sorry, you aren't interesting enough," then just walk away? And if reporters can do that, why can't anybody else? Wouldn't that be great?

"Oh, sorry, Aunt Bernice, but you're just boring the living shit out of me right now and the thought of having to stand here while you continue to flap your lips about why you don't think God intended for us to eat cheese is just, well, unbearable. I gotta take a shit, anyway, so later, okay?"

I'd know to add in that extra made-up detail about having to take a shit. You know, just to help her save some face and all. No need to be mean about it. But, holy shit, that would be great if we could do that in real life. Annie says I can always find the good story in anybody when I want to, and not to sound all braggy, but I know what she means. To be honest, I do believe every single person has at least one really good story in them. The hard part is to ask the right questions and help them find and let it out. A lot of the time it's not even the story they start telling you that's good, it's a little side road that's the good stuff. "There's your story right there!" I've said more than once. But nobody ever takes that well. They hate being told that their favourite pet story about themselves is a piece of boring shit. I don't get that at all. I mean, why not be happy that at least you actually do have a story in you that someone would find interesting, even if it's not the one you think it should be? Annie says it's something about you having been able to embarrass them from the past, present and future, and all at once. What?

"If it's their pet story," explained Annie, "then they've been pulling it out for years by now, telling it every time they can. So you're making them feel like they've been an idiot already, before." And how is that my fault?

I'd be a reporter if it meant I'd be allowed to hold up my hands and say, "Stop right there. That's some boring shit you're telling there. Just answer my questions, and I'll let you know when you say something good. Let me help you be interesting, okay?" Hell, yeah. I want to be a reporter now for sure.

Dad always says everyone has a backstory. I know I'm lucky that Dad lets me drive around with him when he works taking care of bad people sometimes. For the first few months I stayed in the car but the boredom was so bad, I almost wanted to go to school. Almost. I learned the entire inside of that car over the first few weeks. I had examined everything. I started first with the obvious stuff, like the glove compartment, which reminds me. Why do they call it the glove compartment? I mean, if I had gloves I wouldn't be leaving them in a car. Shouldn't you be wearing them if you're lucky enough to have gloves? I've looked in a lot of glove compartments and I've never even once found a pair of gloves in any of them. Lots of other interesting stuff, but never gloves. The one in Dad's car has a whole bunch of stuff crammed into it, including a book on how to work every single part of his car. How to "troubleshoot" if something suddenly stops working, how to make the windows roll up and down (if you're a moron, I guess?) how to make sure the tires are the right "pressure," and even a page that thanks you for buying the car in the first place. That make made laugh a bit. I mean you already bought it, right? So what's with the suck-up job after the fact? I got so bored sitting in that car, I even started reading every single scrap of paper I could find in that flap above the driver's seat, the one where Dad has tiny pieces of papers with notes on them. I like to read them and then make up a story about what they mean. You know, figure out their "backstory," as Dad would say. One time I read, "$50 Ben no more," and decided it meant that a Ben owed my dad fifty dollars and if he didn't pay it, he would be no more. As in, wouldn't breathe anymore. Then I tried to figure out why he had borrowed that fifty dollars in the first place and why he couldn't pay it back. By the time I was finished, I felt so bad for Ben, I almost asked my dad to please give the guy a break and let him go. I also found 87 cents in the car, just from rummaging around the cracks in the seats. Bingo, right? But waiting around in the car gives me time to wonder about this Ben guy's backstory, too. Dad says backstories are what make people good or bad since it's what we do with our "situation," as Dad likes to call it, that makes us a good or bad person. I asked my sister Ruth what her backstory was one time, trying to sound cool, I guess, and tight with Dad. I was waiting for her to ask me what backstory meant so I could fake surprise, then say how it's something me and Dad know about.

But instead she looked at me and said, "The fuck is wrong with you?"

"It's something Dad said…"

I know she's just jealous that Dad sometimes takes me to work with him.

"He's just letting you wait in the car," says Ruth kind of meanly. "That's not the same as letting you watch him at work."

I know I shouldn't have but I instantly bragged that she was wrong, that I did get to watch Dad on the job. I heard someone call him the Enforcer one time and I wanted to tell them that they were wrong. Once my dad is making a work-related visit it's kind of too late. He's already decided you aren't going to do what you're supposed to. Whatever that is. When I asked Mom what an enforcer is she pretended not to hear me. So I pretended that I never asked the question.

"I swear I smelled blood!"

Ruth stared at me for a minute.

"You must have dreamed that," she said. "That's just crazy talk. No one would believe that for a second, and will just think you're a troublemaking liar."

I should have let it go but I couldn't. Calling me a liar? I'm maybe used to Nanny and Mom saying that to me but I knew Ruth knew it was true. Ruth tells me that telling dreams like they're truths can get you into big trouble.

"And then no more dreams for you."

Maybe she's right. Maybe I dreamt the whole thing? Maybe I'm really at school and not with Dad on the job, but I'm so bored at my desk I'm dreaming with my eyes open? Maybe this dreaming business has something to do with what Nanny says about how a sheep spends its whole life being scared of wolves, only to be eaten by the shepherd in the end. I don't know why the Lord's shepherd is eating sheep; those things look so thick I don't even know how you'd begin to take a bite of the damn thing. But next time I'm watching Dad while he works, I'm going to try and remember to pinch myself. See if I wake up in French class.

One thing I know about my dad for sure, though, and this isn't any part of some dream, is how he always says if you're gonna hurt someone when it's personal, so no one is paying you 'cause it's not part of the job, you want to make sure they taste like a terrified pig just before it gets slaughtered. Or something like that. Dad always says it so much better than I can remember when I want to repeat it. He's the most perfect storyteller I know. But I think it means you don't try and calm them down when they first see the gun, or knife, or baseball bat. Nope. Let them scare themselves so much that they'll taste pretty bad and shit their pants even before they die. Or something like that. I don't think Dad meant he would eat a person, of course, dead or alive. I wonder if my dad and his brother got their gift of fighting and holding grudges so long from their dad? I know it wasn't from Nanny. She thinks punishment is something only God is allowed to do.

"Why does only God get to fight back?" I asked her one time. "How come only He gets to do the whole revenge thing?"

"That's not true," said Nanny.

Then she talked about an eye for an eye, a kick in the balls for a kick in the balls, and so on for the next half hour. Okay, I made that last part up, about the balls. But as it turns out, apparently even God agrees you need to push back. And even God says if someone shits on you, you get to shit back on them. Twice. I like that.

"How come God doesn't plot more against the really bad people?" I asked Nanny one time.

That was back when I was a lot younger and didn't know any better. Back when I believed what Nanny said about sinners. But I still think it was a good question. I mean, I get the whole story about wanting us to have free will, blah, blah, just to see what we'll do with it and that whole idea about what do we do when we think nobody is watching. Or something.

"The Lord doesn't have to 'plot,' " said Nanny. "He can just make it happen."

Right. Hallelujah. I can just make it happen, too. Eventually. If I plan it right.

"You can't do anything to Uncle Luther," says Annie.

She's my favourite sister. Hell, she's my favourite person. But she doesn't know a whole lot about the importance of payback.

"Payback costs you more than the person you go after," says Annie. "It hurts you more than it hurts them."

31

It will never hurt me, I think to myself, but if it does, some pain is definitely worth more than others. I smile reassuringly at Annie, wanting to make her think her words have landed where they need to be.

"I hear you," I say, though I know she's wrong, of course. Fighting back is never a bad thing. But I want Annie to think I believe her.

"No, you don't, you bullshitter," says Annie, and we both laugh and change the subject.

I know it worries and stresses Annie out whenever I talk about my list of "Shit-Heads-I-Owe-Big-Time." Unlike peaceful Annie, and plotting-me, our older sister Ruth jokes about taking a machine gun to them in one really loud end.

"Herd them all into the Legion and take them all out in one noisy blast," says Ruth. "It'd be all over in ten seconds!"

That's one of the things I like about Ruth. She's direct and upfront. Ruth won't punch you in the head when you're not looking or wait until you least expect it. If she hates you, you know it. If she's mad at you, you know right away. But nope, not for me. I want to make it as unexpected and slow as possible. Like Dad said, so they'd taste terrible if anyone took so much as a lick off one of them. None of that shit about hitting the ground before they even knew what hit them, either. I want them to know it's me. I want them to know what I'm about to do before I do it. I want them to know that I'm not just gonna scream anymore the next time they try to hurt me.

"People can read your Irish thoughts from across the room," says Dad.

So yeah, I gotta work on that. I need to get that perfect blank face my sister Julia has mastered. But as much as I enjoy thinking about it and plotting, sometimes I worry about jinxing myself. You know, let myself believe it's really going to happen. Nanny calls it borrowing happiness from the future.

"That's like begging God to knock you over," says Nanny. "You're just tempting Him and the Devil to teach you a Big One. Don't be happy until you know you can be happy."

Ruth has a different idea about that. She says Nanny is wrong and so are all the other sad sacks out there. When I told her that sometimes I'm afraid to be happy and reminded her about Nanny's warnings against borrowing happiness from the future, Ruth said you can't screw yourself up in the future just because you allow yourself to imagine being happy one day. She says if you don't have hope why else would those little dark kids on TV with those pregnant-looking bellies and flies walking on their faces not kill themselves, if they don't have hope. And if they can have hope, then everybody can have hope.

"And you *should* count your chickens before they're hatched," says Ruth. "You should put all your eggs in one basket. The whole point is to feel excited and look forward to something. If you lose or your wish doesn't ever come true, okay, you'll be disappointed for a day. But until then, you get to feel all hopeful and happy and excited until that day."

I wonder when Ruth stopped doing that. When did she stop believing it for herself? She gave up counting her chickens before they hatched a long time ago.

Chapter Three

One day our cousin Lucy showed up with her fancy black leather shoes that she likes to shine the tips of each night before going to bed, and a real suitcase, like a movie star, stuffed with fancy clothing and a mountain of underwear and socks. It's like someone famous is moving in with us. Her mom had to leave because she knows that one day Uncle Oscar will kill her. One time Lucy asked Ruth if her dad had ever touched any of us girls in a bad way and Ruth said later she was secretly worried Lucy was fishing 'cause she wanted to claim our dad had maybe touched her, something which all of us would know is a lie.

"So I just point-blank asked," says Ruth, "No, your dad never touched any of us girls. He was always kind and generous with all of us. Every Easter he gives each of us a basket filled with candies and 100 pennies. We always get to feel rich for weeks with all of our new pennies in our Easter baskets. But why are you asking? Did our dad ever, you know… touch you?"

Lucy looks horrified and instantly starts saying no, no way, our dad has never touched her like that at all, of course! Then realizing, I guess, that her way of asking had made Ruth think she was about to make some terrible claim, tries to explain why she had asked.

"When I was almost 12 my dad had come into my room one night, drunk, and crawled into bed with me."

Ruth was so caught off guard she didn't know what to say. So she just waited for Lucy to continue talking and finish her terrible story.

"And I looked at him and told him to 'GET OUT, DAD!' and he did."

"Wow," said Ruth. "Then what happened?"

"I told all my girlfriends to be careful around my dad from then on."

After Lucy's mom ran away and left her all alone, our mom decided that a 13-year-old girl needs to be living with other girls, not alone with just a dad and two brothers. The day after she moved in Lucy managed to end up with her own special drawer in the dresser in the basement for her collection of underwear and socks. Mom tells us we aren't allowed to touch them.

"Those are just for Lucy."

Mom always talks about Lucy like Lucy can't hear her or speak for herself even when she's standing right there not two feet away from her. Lucy's underwear looks brand new and made just for kids. For fancy 13-year-old girls. I didn't know underwear could come in colours other than white. But Lucy has not only white ones, she also has blue, pink and even purple ones. Some have white lace around the opening of the legs and at least one pair has tiny ponies on the front. Her socks are just as interesting and fancy, too. Lucy is so easy to hate. She has her own special comb too, for her long, curly red hair. Everyone is always saying how beautiful it is, making me feel like it was me who chose to have pale straight hair. It's not my fault I don't have colour or curls. And like Nanny would say, it's not like Lucy got to pick her curls or colour, either. So why does everyone treat her like a princess? Like, she's so smart and all? I'd have picked her hair if God had let me do the picking when I was about to be born, too.

"You can borrow stuff from my drawer anytime you want to," Lucy says to me and Annie and Ruth when Mom isn't around.

"And my comb, too!"

She holds it out in front of her. It's a dark pink and has a small white and blue unicorn on the edge with teeny sparkles on its horn that when you hold it near the light, shines and glitters like hidden diamonds.

"That's just stupid." I regret it as soon as the words leave my mouth.

"What?" asks Lucy. She looks confused. "What's stupid? My… comb?"

Of course, now I have to stand my ground no matter what.

"Yes," says Ruth. "The comb. It's stupid."

I try not to glow too hard in the face of Ruth's support. I know she's lying just like me. We've both played with that dumb comb a million times when Lucy isn't around. One time her father, Uncle Oscar, came and picked her up for the day and the second the door closed behind her we were all running to her dresser drawer, yelling.

"No, I dibs it first!"

It actually is a bit of stupid comb, though. It hurt to pull through my hair. But I knew my hair was better for it having shared the comb's sharp teeth with a princess. I always had to force myself not to break it into pieces before putting it back, though.

"Don't do anything to the comb." Ruth eyed me when I finally got my turn after her and Annie. It's weird how she can read my mind sometimes.

"A comb can't be stupid," says Lucy. Her voice is a bit shaky. She's looking down at her dumb comb now, no longer holding it out.

"Unicorns are for babies," I say.

"I'm not a baby," says Lucy.

We all just stare at her. I want to call her a baby-la-la. So I do.

Later, when we all got lice and had to get our heads practically shaved, I could hear Lucy sobbing in the bathroom. To be fair, though, she didn't say a word as Mom chopped those long curls off, telling Lucy the whole time that it would grow back and that she was going to look so cute with short hair and that everybody was going to be able to see those big beautiful eyes of hers for a change and she better appreciate it while it was short because before she knew it, that hair would be past her butt again and once more she'd be complaining about sitting on it and how long it takes to comb and keep nice. I was waiting for Mom to take a breath. Cutting off our hair took a couple of minutes and Mom didn't waste any time talking about it, either. Our shitty hair filled with nits just fell onto the ground as Mom snipped us all down to practically skin in the yard. The rats would be running off with our dirty hair before morning to make nests for their babies. At least I know now how rats get lice. They catch it from Point people who weren't so lucky, I guess.

Lucy still wasn't saying anything as Mom took the scissors to her, dropping each large section as she cut through it into a small bucket she had placed close by. Lucy wasn't going to look like a boy like the rest of us once Mom was done. She was just going to look like a totally different little girl. One who has hair that stops just short of her ears, in a perfectly straight line. Mom had attached a line of scotch tape to Lucy's hair and was following the top line of the tape perfectly. As the hair was placed into the bucket it still had the tape attached. I wondered what Mom was planning to do with it afterwards. The rats weren't going to get Lucy's hair. Once the cutting was done, she then pulled Lucy in close and started carefully pulling the nit comb through her now short hair.

"It's okay!" said Mom when Lucy flinched. "I'll go more slowly, sorry."

Mom must have spent a good hour or more just slowly pulling that nit comb through every strand of Lucy's hair, sometimes stopping to give her a tight hug and tell her how brave she was being and what a gorgeous girl she is, no matter what. I looked at the bucket and wondered if I'd be able to light it on fire and not get caught. At least not until a good pile of it had all burned up.

Lucy still wasn't saying anything, wasn't even looking upset or nothing anymore. She just stood there, like a tall doll, while Mom worked on her hair. Once Mom was done, she patted Lucy on the shoulders and said she was perfect.

"You're good to go now. Not a thing moving in that hair anymore at all."

After that, Lucy stopped cleaning the tips of her black leather shoes before going to bed. Now she just shoves them over to the side after she takes them off before hopping into bed. Later, I had to swear to Ruth it wasn't me who broke the comb into three pieces, either. Ever since her haircut, Lucy has asked us to call her "Ginger" and is always hanging around Mom while she holds Hanna or reads to Beth. Mom will look up from her book and motion for Lucy to sit with her. She even hangs out with Mom when she's hanging stuff out on the clothesline in the middle of winter off the back balcony. What a suck-up. I can hear her telling Mom she should let her hang the wet stuff up on the line so Mom's fingers won't turn white. Mom always gives her a quick little hug and tells her what a special little princess she is.

"You know you're like one of my girls, right?" says Mom, and then pulls her close and gives her a squeeze.

"I'm one of your sisters now," Lucy announces to us girls a few days later. "I'm the big sister, too, since I'm older than Ruth."

I know it's mean but it's like I can't help myself. I completely ignore her. Pretend not to hear her. Pretend not to see her. It's not enough for her to have her own rich girl clothes and have our dad think she's the most beautiful girl for miles and miles around. She wants to steal our mother, too.

"Your hair grows so slowly," I say without looking away from my book. It shuts her up for days.

"Want to hear more about 'Devil's Lane'?" asks Lucy one night when Mom's at one of her meetings with the lesbians from McGill. Mom is forever trying to figure out how to fix what's wrong in the Point. She says the housing and education and welfare are complete shit. Her and a gang of other moms in the neighbourhood keep yelling about it and marching up and down the streets, waving at the television cameras whenever they show up, sounding like fancy people from Westmount or Ville LaSalle when the microphone gets shoved in front of one of their faces. I hate to admit it but Mom is pretty brave. Or is really good at faking it. She never acts scared when the riot squad shows up to force them off the mayor's lawn or out of the hallway of the welfare offices. She tells us to go limp when the police try to drag us out of the building but I feel stupid doing that and just slowly crawl along the floor as they drag everyone else out. I always worry that someone is going to step on my hands or fall on my head. Fixing shit is hard work, right?

"You need to do what's right," Mom will say to the police officers as she's lifted out of the hallway. "And you know what that is!"

I'm always surprised that the cops don't drop her on purpose or hurt her. Mom says it's on account of the media being there. "They're witnesses to the cause," says Mom. As much as she bugs the living shit out of me half the time, I know she means that stuff when she says it. She'd even do it if they did drop her on her head or drag her body down the hallways of the welfare offices. "You don't do stuff because there's no risk or cost," says Mom. "You do it because someone has to do it. So why not you?"

Sometimes a few dads will show up and join the group. A few brothers and boyfriends, too. I think I even saw Garfield one time, this kid who doesn't even live in the Point but seems to love it for some weird reason. He has a lot of friends in the neighbourhood so is often around, hanging out, buying everybody pizza. I think he's rich, too. But I try not to hold that against him. I like his dark hair. He always smiles at everyone and acts all friendly all the time.

"Men can definitely play a role in the movement," says Mom. "Their support is important, just as long as they understand their role."

Which, according to Mom, is to stand around and look pretty. "They need to leave all the talking to us."

Lucy is asking again if we want to hear about Devil's Lane. Okay, she knows how to get us.

"Sure, okay."

I don't want to sound too eager, even though I'm dying for Lucy to tell me more about Devil's Lane. She's been telling us stories about Devil's Lane ever since the second night she first moved in here and realized that none of us wanted her socks, underwear or comb. But a good story? And a scary one at that?

"You want to call the other girls?"

Lucy is finally starting to figure out how it works around here. We share practically everything and if there's not enough to go around, well, we just don't want it then. She's letting me be the one to give my sisters the gift of the story, even if I'm not the one who is gonna tell it, by being the one to call them.

"LUCY'S GONNA TELL US ABOUT DEVIL'S LANE!"

I yell, knowing it'll bring everyone running, no matter what they're doing or where they are. And instantly I can hear the toilet flushing, the TV being turned off, and someone running up the stairs from the basement. In a couple of minutes, we're all ready to crowd onto Mom's bed and listen up. Lucy reminds us to turn off all the lights first, and Hanna starts to cry. Annie pulls her close and reminds her, it's just a story. It's not real. Hanna is so happy to be getting a cuddle with Annie, she soon settles down and we know she'll be asleep before Lucy even gets to the scariest parts.

"The real secret to making it safely through Devil's Lane to the other side is first making yourself let go of everything you care about before you begin; even before taking that first step," says Lucy. "You have to stop caring about *everything*."

See what I mean? That girl can tell a story. The only problem is when you're trying to tell a story to six different girls all at the same time, especially us six girls, even before you can say the next sentence, they're going to want to pick apart and discuss the first sentence. And ask about a million questions, too.

"Wait a minute," says Annie. "When you say 'everything you care about,' do you mean even stuff like, you know, breathing? Do you have to let go of, you know, breathing? Or are you talking more about the food and people you care about? Favourite toys and books and shirts and so on?"

You can't say stuff like that around Annie. She believes everyone has to be very exact with what they say. I think she needs these kinds of details to feel sure about stuff. To know what exactly to believe is true. What's real.

"Of course she doesn't mean you can't breathe, for God's sake!" says Ruth. "Don't be talking like a fool!"

Uh oh. Ruth is using Nanny's voice. And with Annie.

"Don't call me a fool," says Annie. "Why would you say that?"

"A fool is a fool," says Ruth.

Lucy is obviously not used to having her stories interrupted.

"Wait! Wait! Wait, girls!" she says, holding up her hands.

Big mistake.

"Don't tell us what to do," says Ruth.

"You aren't the boss of us," I toss in.

"No, no, no," says Lucy. "I'm just saying maybe you guys should just let me, you know, tell the story… and then, maybe ask the questions afterwards?"

Ask questions afterwards? Afterwards? You can tell Lucy has spent a lot of years growing up alone. Or at least invisible. In our family, the question part is maybe the best part of hearing a new story. In fact, if no one has any questions it means it's probably a shit story hardly worth telling.

"Fine," says Annie. "I'll be quiet, go ahead. Tell the story. I'm listening."

Which means Annie is now about to close her ears so tightly she wouldn't be able to hear if you suddenly screamed that a family of sewer rats has just arrived and is setting up camp in the kitchen.

"Oh, okay," says Lucy. And she starts again.

"The real trick to making it past all the…"

I can't help but feel a little sorry for Lucy. Our love isn't enough. Our mother's love isn't enough. Living with us and having our dad think her hair is more beautiful than any of ours is not enough. She wants to be like us. She wants to be one of us. She doesn't know yet that she can never be one of us. She's a rich girl, forever, no matter where she goes. It's a stink she'll never be able to throw off.

"When is Lucy going back to where she came from?" I asked Mom one day. For a second I thought she was going to slap me.

"DON'T you say that! Don't you dare!"

"I didn't say anything. I just asked when is she going…" Mom's verbal slap didn't really hurt but it made me jump a little.

"Just shut up about it!" she hissed quietly, looking around as if she were afraid maybe Lucy was hiding under one of the chairs or perched in the corner, listening to my question about when she was finally going away.

Nanny told me one time that you can't have everything. She's wrong. Lucy has everything. Months later, after Lucy moves away again, we wait a few days before we look in her special drawer. Everything is gone. It took a few days but finally I had to ask.

"Mom? When is Lucy coming back?"

"Why?"

"Well, you know, the girls miss her and stuff."

"Hmmph," said Mom.

When Hanna, Beth and Julia all asked Mom at dinner where was Lucy and when was she coming back, Mom seemed angry.

"Why? It's not like any of you were ever nice to her. All she ever wanted was for you girls to like her and let her love you. But all of your petty jealousies and meanness finally did the poor girl in. She's gone, don't ask about her again."

She's gone? Like, forever? We know we can't ask Mom any more questions but when we all got together that night on Mom's bed after she left for one of her meetings we agreed we'd all be nicer if Lucy ever comes back. But seriously, how could she think we don't love her? Maybe we don't always like her, but she can tell a story like nobody else.

Starting tomorrow I get to miss 11 days of school and I can't wait. It's the beginning of selling poppies week for the Legion and although I hate selling the poppies, I love that my teachers can't bitch about it since they'd look like they hate war veterans and don't support the Canadian Legion and the soldiers who still do important stuff in other countries. When Dad heard about how my English teacher called home to complain to Mom, he went down to the school to smooth it all over.

"I can't imagine what could be taking place in the classroom next week that is more important than showing our support of those who made the ultimate sacrifice," said Dad with one of his warmest smiles, one of those that reach his eyes and always make the other person grin back. Well, until now.

He was thrown off at first, he explained later, when instead of apologizing for the phone call, my English teacher went red in the face and then tried to shut the whole thing down.

"Every poppy represents the failure of political leaders to avoid war. Wearing one and honouring the dead implicitly endorses the type of idiocy that led to the deaths to begin with," she said.

My dad must have been astonished. My teacher is young and pretty, but his magic didn't work with her. Dad admits it took a while for his brain to catch up. To realize he had one of those "war haters" sitting in front of him.

"The poppy is a symbol of peace," said Dad, "and wearing one is a way to honour the fallen to achieve that peace."

He was surprised when that still didn't shut it down. But then again, my English teacher is really smart and knows what she thinks and isn't afraid to say so. Dad's good looks weren't going to be enough that day in the office. The teacher wasn't even halfway done explaining why she thought it was not only stupid for me to miss a week of school, but also for the *wrong* reasons.

"The problem I have with the poppy," she explained to Dad, as if he had actually asked her what her problem with the poppy was, "is that in wearing one we are asked to remember the veterans who died in the wars, but never to demand demilitarization or pacifism. And for you to put a child in that situation, to support *that*?"

Uh oh. She had used that word, the one Dad and his friends down at the Legion really hate. The "p" word.

"I think you've misunderstood the purpose of my coming here today," said Dad, who must have been shocked by the interruption. "This is only a courtesy call."

I got nervous on the teacher's behalf when I heard that part of the conversation. She must have had no clue what she was risking.

"You don't have to like or appreciate it, of course," said Dad. "Just respect *my* decision in this situation. My children will be back in school on November 11th, ready to stand proudly with their classmates and teachers to share in the respectful moment of silence on the 11th day at the 11th hour. Thank you for your time." Then we calmly stood up and walked out of the classroom.

That year, as I shivered on the corner of St. Catherine and Guy, I wondered about my teacher. She had seemed so angry about the whole thing. I kept trying to figure out what exactly had bugged her so much. Why did she hate poppies, exactly? How could such a small red flower say so much? I started noticing that some people would say, "I don't believe in war!" as they brushed past me on the sidewalk. The hell? What's to not believe? I mean, wars aren't unicorns, right? Did they really think that by just saying they don't believe in them, wars will somehow no longer exist? It's like that bullshit question about trees falling in the forest and nobody hearing them.

"Kathy, you can't flip people off. You're representing the Legion while you're out there," said Dad. "The Legion is recognized as the guardians of Remembrance Day in Canada. If you're rude, then the public loses respect for the Legion. No matter what anyone says to you, just smile and say nothing back."

My dad is one to talk, though. The first year I stood on the corner for a straight week selling poppies, I realized why Dad doesn't actually stand out there and sell them himself.

"How much?" asked one older guy.

He had been watching me for a while before finally deciding to talk to me. I figured he thought it was great that a young person was willing to freeze her ass off while raising funds for old guys with missing legs and arms. And dead ones, too.

"Whatever you think is fair." I say my line with a smile.

Dad had given me all kinds of comebacks to anyone who asked how much it cost, what the poppy stood for, or why I was doing it for the Legion.

"Whatever I think is *fair*?" said the old guy back to me with a smile. But not a nice smile. Just one of those gross, creepy old-men kind of smiles. I remembered what Dad had said about representing the Legion and all when I replied.

"Yes, sir. In addition to a remembrance of Canada's war veterans, the funds raised from the sale of poppies go towards helping the vets and their families. It's totally non-profit."

That rarely was enough to make the creepy ones go away. They'd try to hang around, saying creepy shit and looking me up and down until finally, after being ignored long enough, they would go away. Sometimes they'd come back later, though. Like they had thought up some gem they just had to share with me.

"You know, when I look at you…" I learned to just tune them out.

Sometimes I'd get someone more interesting, someone who wanted to actually debate with me the whole idea of poppies being a symbol of evil.

"I realize that poppies have become part of our culture as a symbol of respect for the sacrifices made by fellow Canadians," said one guy. "I totally get that. But…"

What would usually follow was some dumb speech about "forgetting too soon the things we thought we'd never forget," blah, blah, blaaaah. But one day I heard a new one. This guy was even kind of good-looking. Well, in an old person kind of way.

"The military is the best way to eliminate the bottom ten percentage of the population," he said. I liked that he seemed to mean what he was saying and wasn't being creepy at all. I surprised myself by answering him.

"Well, maybe that could become a new weapon," I said. "You know, suggest to the bad guys that they hire everyone for their army. That way we'd be able to get rid of ten percent of them all in one shot!"

I was disappointed when he didn't laugh. Didn't even smile. Instead, he got all boring, like the rest of them.

"It's ridiculous to try and dissociate such a powerful symbol from the politics of war."

Yawn.

"How do you reconcile your claim to be trying to help *anyone*, with the knowledge that the poppy has become a symbol of the militaristic rhetoric and pageantry that is unleashed every Remembrance Day."

Double yawn. Looks aren't everything, I guess.

"By wearing the poppy the solider becomes a martyr and hero."

Triple yawn. I don't even bother rolling my eyes at the invisible audience anymore. Instead, now I collect the dumbest comments and questions of the day to share with my sisters, then make them laugh with what I wish I could have said in return.

"Why don't you just suck yourself off and then jump in front of the metro, asshole?" "You don't believe in war? Well, I don't believe in YOU!"

My sisters agree we should be allowed one "Fuck off!" a day. That, and one solid punch to the throat for the week. Yeah, I can see why our dad doesn't stand on the corner selling poppies.

It would look bad for the Legion.

When I finally go back to school 11 days later it's hard not to feel invisible. Everyone is talking about stuff that doesn't make any sense to me. I mean, not that it was making a whole lot of sense before I left to sell the poppies but still, leaving school for that long feels like I'm never going to catch up. I don't really need school, anyway, I figure. I'm going to be a writer when I grow up and I already know how to write. I've always wanted to be a writer. Okay, that's a lie. I also have wanted to be a police officer, social worker and reporter. Oh, and a teacher. Who wouldn't want to play with chalk, be the boss and yell at kids all day, right? But it feels like I've always wanted to be a writer. Writers are rich and famous and everyone thinks they're smart. But first, before I can become a writer, Mom says I need to finish school.

But before I can finish school, first I'm going to have to pass French.

Passing French includes having to pass the provincial oral exam. I know, it sounds like a fancy blow job, right? "Provincial oral exam." The French teacher has told us to pick a topic we feel we know enough about that no matter what follow-up questions the provincial oral examiner asks, we'll be able to give at least a half-decent answer. Annie says I should talk about my dog. How I got him, how I came up with his name, why I love him, what he likes to eat, how he sleeps next to me in my bed each night, and so on and so forth. Of course, there's only one small problem.

"I don't have a dog," I say to Annie. "I've never had a dog."

Annie has to finish laughing before she can say anything.

"Of course you don't have a dog!" says Annie. "I know that! The point though is to pick a topic you know you can babble on endlessly about with details. Lots and lots of boring details so the guy goes into a half-coma and is secretly begging you to shut up in his head!"

See what I mean? Annie is a genius.

"Mon chien est un bon chien. Il a trois ans et il est noir comme la nuit. Il est bien porté et presque jamais aboyer, sauf si un fucking rat apparaît bien sûr, puis il aboie sa tête folle. Mais ça va, je l'aime quand même. C'était mon père qui m'a acheté mon chien. Il m'a dit que son nom était Blaze et Bonne Fête. J'adore mon adorable chien. J'adore mon Papa."

Hell, I can make this shit up all day. I maybe might pass grade seven after all. No matter what that provincial examiner asks me, I'm going to be able to pull one of those statements out of my ass and just babble away.

Ruth is being weird with flies again. I caught a glimpse of her jar and I guess she saw the look on my face.

"At least I don't eat them, right?"

The fuuuuck.

"No, seriously," says Ruth. "I just transform them. They don't die, they just aren't flies anymore."

"What do you mean… 'transform' them?"

I can't help myself. I have to ask. I gotta poke that with a stick.

"I make them more special," says Ruth.

Jesus, ever since she's moved back from Nanny's place she creeps me out half the time. If she's not speaking in tongues or praising the Lord, and I swear to god she does that shit in her room knowing we can hear her and is just trying to freak us out, she's fucking with insects like a goddamn serial killer, practicing on something small first. For years she had me scared she was a vampire. This feels even worse.

"No really," she says. "Now instead of being annoying and making that really irritating buzzing sound, flying all around the room and shitting and puking on your food, they're something totally new, minus all the parts that make people hate flies. You don't have to hate these ones!"

Ruth is being serious. She thinks by having carefully ripped off their wings she's made them something she can control now. Something everyone won't hate anymore. She's wrong. They're disgusting. It was bad enough to see them buzzing around the room. But now? Racing around the bottom of her jar, all frantic and crawling over each other? Just, eww.

"Ruth?"

I gotta at least try, right?

"Flies that can't fly are just fucking weird." Also, she's being… I don't even know. But I act like this is a serious conversation.

"That's like a dog that can't bark or shit. It's just not normal. Just squish them and be done. Why are you torturing a bunch of damn flies?"

I knew I had gone too far. Said too much. As much as Ruth bugs the living shit out of me, I know her strength is fake. She's weaker than she wants us all to know. She hides behind her mean words for strength and to hide her soft parts.

"Oh, like YOU know anything!" she laughs meanly. "Do you want to know what Nanny calls you? What MOM calls you?"

See what I mean? She's going in for the kill now. I'm about to be destroyed. Ruth is that baby rat in the corner everyone underestimates, thinking it's not really a serious threat until it's bigger. Much bigger. And, of course, they're wrong.

"Sure," I say, trying to act like I don't give a shit.

"Well, wouldn't you like to know!" she says.

Now I'm not sure if she made it all up or just changed her mind about crushing me.

"Why did Mom and her family eat their rats when she was little?" I ask.

Yup, change the subject. Give Ruth something to be all bossy and know-it-all about. I know why they ate the rats, of course. I've only heard

47

about it a zillion times. And they sure weren't the only family eating rats in the Point at that time, either. But it's one of Ruth's favourite stories to tell. And to be honest, it's one she tells really well.

"If you think about how Grandpa dealt with the rats in his basement, how he hunted them, you can tell he wasn't stupid," says Ruth.

Then just when I'm worried she sounds a little too impressed, even filled with respect or awe, she clarifies everything.

"A perv? Sure. Mean and cruel? Yup, okay, right. But he was pretty clever, too."

Ruth is just warming up. If Annie had been there, I would have moved my lips to match the stuff coming out of Ruth's mouth. Thank god Annie isn't there. Why does anyone think being clever gives anybody a pass for anything, ever?

"He used to fish them right out of that hole he had in the kitchen floor on Liverpool Street," continues Ruth. "I swear that's why half of Mom's siblings, including her father, ended up all crazy and mixed up and mean. Sewer rats are loaded with lead and pus and all kinds of disease. You aren't supposed to eat them. I mean, you can, of course, but you have to boil them and cook them at a really high heat first or they'll make you sick."

Ruth misunderstands the look on my Irish face.

"Hey, I'm not judging him!" she says. "At least not for that. They were all starving to death and I'm sure he thought it was better than seeing his kids hungry all the time. He was just trying to feed his family. He didn't know he was poisoning everyone."

I wonder what a rat would taste like. They seem like they'd be too hairy and crunchy and wet and ugly to eat. What would it look like if you barfed it back up? Do you eat the tail? What about those scratchy and cruel looking claws?

"Did they eat the whole thing?" I ask Ruth.

I know she's thrilled to have a question, to be able to take her story further and enrich it with more details.

"You shouldn't eat the head," she says. "That's where the worst of the poison is. It's all in the brains. That's where the saying 'shit for brains' comes from, actually."

Not sure about that.

"Of course, eating squirrels can turn you into a zombie on account of their meat making holes in your brain and all, but rats? Under strict rules, they can be okay to eat."

I know she's making half of that stuff up. But she's another one who does tell a story well. She is practically humming now, sending prayers up to heaven that I'll ask about those "strict rules."

"What about the tail?" I ask. "What did they do with the tail?"

"Not even a cat will eat the tail of a rat," says Ruth. "But Grandpa liked to chew on it while he listened to the radio. Says it helped to keep his teeth clean."

I stand there processing this. Grandpa did keep his teeth for a long time. There's a lot of status attached to getting your first set of chompers in the Point but Grandpa never had enough money to buy himself a set. So maybe the tail being good for cleaning teeth was true and Ruth wasn't making that up just to scare me. I mean, Grandpa did get to keep his teeth for as long as I can remember. Mind you, they looked like short little dirty tree stumps in his mouth, but yeah, they were his. They were real.

"And the hands and feet?" I asked. "What about the hands and feet?"

Ruth paused. I can tell she's trying to cook up a good but fast one for that.

"Grandpa made jewellery out of the paws. He made each of his daughters a bracelet for Christmas one year. He said it would be a reminder of where they came from. Keep them humble."

That I know for sure is made up. If Mom had a bracelet somewhere made up of rats' paws I would have definitely seen it by now. But see what I mean? Ruth is a great storyteller. She should be writing her stories down. I know she does really well in her English class at Westmount High School. Even though nobody at the school ever talks to her or Annie on account of them being white trash from the Point and all, her English teacher thinks she's great. And not just because she's never rude or loud or swearing a lot like me all the time. Nope, Ruth is polite and respectful but she's also smart in her own way, and a different way from Annie.

49

"I don't know math all that much," says Ruth, but she's just being polite about Annie being the best one in our family when it comes to math. I think Ruth believes it's kind of rude to try and be too good at something when someone else is already the best, right? But she can give that to Annie 'cause no one else in the family is even close when it comes to writing poems like Ruth does. Shit, I didn't even think she cared all that much really about writing until she came home one day all blushy and in a good mood and said Mr. McGinty had loved one of her poems.

"Can I read it?"

I knew I had made a mistake the second the words came out of my mouth. Ruth couldn't risk me fucking up her happiness so of course she wasn't going to let me read it. At least not yet. Even though I would have been super careful not to say the wrong thing, there was no way she could risk it. First, she had to let Mr. McGinty's love for her words cook a little longer and totally sink in.

"I can tell you about it, though," she said. She could tell I was disappointed and I could tell my disappointment added to her joy in the moment.

"We had to write an essay about a book we read in English class. *Lord of the Flies*. We've been reading it all term, sometimes alone and sometimes Mr. McGinty would read it out loud in class."

I hadn't read it but of course Ruth would somehow get to read a book about flies and from the title it sounds like these are flies that are lording it over everybody. Jesus. Sounds like a sick book. Bossy flies. No wonder she loved it, right?

"The story is all about what happens when people don't have rules in place to force them to be nice and kind and know to share stuff with those who are... weaker," says Ruth. "People who have... less."

Oh, so not a single fly in the whole book? Fancy books like that are so stupid. Why do they want to trick you with a title that says one thing but then you start reading it, and sure enough, not a fly to be found. Maybe that's what got Ruth reading it in the first place, though? The promise of a bunch of bossy flies?

"It's about a bunch of kids who are in a plane crash and end up on a deserted island with no adults around and they get to run the island on their own," says Ruth. "No grown-ups. No rules. It's about what they do when they don't have to worry about anybody looking. How if you feed hatred you don't have to start a war; they'll just kill each other off for you instead."

A bunch of kids in a plane crash? Well, first off, these must be rich kids, right? I mean, I don't know anybody ever who has gone on a plane anywhere, kid or adult. So these are rich kids.

"So? What do they do? Build a boat and row back to wherever they came from?"

I'm half kidding, of course, but my answer seems to have annoyed Ruth so she folds up her paper and starts to leave the room.

"Wait! Aren't you gonna tell me about your poem?"

Ruth looks at me for a second.

"Maybe later," and she leaves the room.

Later, when I know she's going to be away for a while, I look for her poem and I find it. All crunched up under some dirty clothes in the closet of the basement. I unfold it and press down on all of the creases and folds, trying to make it nice and flat and straight. She's got a title at the top of the page. I didn't know people gave their poems a title. Or maybe just Ruth does? She's called it, "Lord of the Flies." Copycat, right? I sit on the floor of the closet and read it softly out loud just to myself:

Lord of the Flies
By Ruth Nora Dobson
November 1972
Mr. McGinty
Grade 9

The Beasties walk to and fro,
never coming back
not having to go.
The Mountain's pace, although slack,
sees the Beasties, never looking back.
As storming seas, with billowing caps
swelling, frothing, for the chance,

to catch the People unaware,
is the Beasties final Victory.
The running People, they all walk.
Cause if they run,
the Beasties stalk.
People running, know they won't
see the Dawning if they wait.
Revenge in their hearts,
and fear in their eyes,
we the People begin to hide.
The Beasties we pray, shall never arrive.
Because,
you see,
if they do,
we, the People
shall surely
die.

I put the paper down and start to cry. I feel like an idiot 'cause I don't even know why and I just can't stop. My chest feels like a heavy cat is sitting on it. Ruth has written short stories before and a few that she's even read out loud to us sometimes, but never any of her poems. Those she always hides away. She wrote a story one time about a girl in a wheelchair who wanted to be a dancer and no matter what, even though she knew she'd never be able to get out of that chair, she kept on wanting to be a dancer. When I asked Ruth why the girl wouldn't just smarten up and stop torturing herself with ideas about the impossible, Ruth just got mad.

"Why do you want to be a paralegal?" I ask Ruth. Like me, she changes her mind all the time but unlike me, she usually has a good reason when she does and I don't get why she doesn't want to be a writer too.

"I'll be able to stop people from being treated unfairly," says Ruth. "I'll be able to help them use the courts to fight their landlords instead of having to live in Shitsville without any way of making them change the wiring and get rid of the roaches and sewer rats."

When I ask Ruth what's the difference between a paralegal and a lawyer, she says one is smart and rich; the other isn't as smart or rich. I don't want to push my luck so I don't ask her which is which. Ruth loves to read at least as much as I do and has even worked in two different libraries. The People's Library in the Point and now a library near Westmount High. So she can get a hold of almost any book she wants now. I'm surprised we don't get along better since we both love books so much. But then again, we don't seem to read the same stuff even when we do.

"I hated *Catcher in the Rye*," says Ruth. "That little freak picking and popping his pimples on the train."

When I try to push her to explain it a bit more she says, "These are ugly people and I don't like them. Who needs to read about other people's miseries, anyway?"

Ruth sent off one of her short stories about a fox that gets caught in a trap to *Redbook* magazine and didn't we all about shit our pants when she got a card from them a few months later. The small printed part on the back said they were delighted to have been able to read her submission but regret it did not fit their current editorial needs. But underneath that someone had written, "Keep writing, this is a terrific and moving short story." Ruth kept that card in her pocket for days and days and I'd see her pulling it out sometimes just to read it again and again when she thought no one was watching. As far as I know, she still has it in her pocket. When I asked her if she had shown it to her boyfriend, Mr. McGinty, she looked like she was going to smack me.

But to be honest, as good as she is with poems and short stories, she's an even better artist. She draws and paints stuff so good, they look like she took a picture. It makes her mad for some reason if you tell her that, though.

"You could be an artist when you grow up!" I told her one time after I saw her drawing of Bambi.

"Naw, I'm going to be a nurse," she says.

"A nurse? You can't be a nurse. That's what Annie is going to do! And you already said you're gonna be a paralegal!"

"So what if Annie becomes a nurse? That doesn't mean I can't be one too," says Ruth.

"But, you gotta do your own dream," I say. "You have to come up with your own ideas!"

"Why?" says Ruth. "Annie already figured it out. Why can't I just copy her? Plus, there's different sorts of nurses."

"You don't have to be an artist, fine. But what about being a vet? You love animals. You could be a doctor for them."

I figure it would be rude to make a joke at this moment about what she does to the flies in her thick glass jar under her bed. But hey, what do I know? Maybe that's what all vets do before they go to school to learn how to be one. Find some small animal to mess with and practice on? You know, transform them and shit?

"I only like dogs," says Ruth. "Little dogs. The ones rich people have. They have cute names and love everyone and bark like crazy if they're not happy. If they don't like something, you know it for sure. That's why people call them yappy. But really, they should just call them happy."

That's Ruth for you. She wants to be yappy. Actually, she already is yappy. That's a perfect description of Ruth. I can't wait to tell Annie that Ruth is yappy. Like one of them fancy little rich-people dogs. I don't know if vets can work with only one kind of an animal, though. I think they take an oath to fix all the cats and dogs and even rats if someone brings one to their clinic for help.

Vets probably don't help rats, though. There's a homeless guy who would sometimes hang out in the Point who was famous for his tree of rats. He'd catch the sewer rats alive so he could hang them from the tree by their mouths, their tails hanging down, and they'd be wiggling and trying to break free until the feral cats from the surrounding laneways would come for them and pick them off that tree like free berries. A single rat can shit fifty times in a day—I've heard Mom say that about a million times—so that tree had a mountain at its base. At first the fresh shit looks like wet black putty, then in a few days it becomes dry and hard and turns grey. When the cats first show up, they circle the dusty base for a few minutes before they attack, staring up at the unexpected feast just waiting to be picked off like low-hanging fruit. The first time I watched them I wondered how I could free the rats. While the cats slowly circle through the mound of grey putty it crumbles and they lose traction. The rats are making a horrible muffled squeaky sound, even though their mouths are somehow tied shut with the way they're hanging from their teeth. Or their jaws? It looks like a small wire or string is looped around their mouth and neck but I can't be sure. I'm afraid to get too close. What if they suddenly manage to pop off? They're wiggling bodies look frantic as they lift their tails and paw at their own faces. It's terrible and I can't look away. Cats are basically chicken shits. Bullies. They'll attack a rat maybe once if they see it in your flat. It's a territorial thing. But most will make that mistake only once. Although they might be able to kill a young one, or maybe one of the stunted rats, most cats quickly learn to avoid a fight with them in the future. Rats are tough suckers and fearless if they feel cornered.

But these alley cats at the Tree of Rats are bold because they know something is wrong with these rats. They can sense they're vulnerable by the terrible sounds they're making and the way they won't stop moving, even though they can't break free of the string that is trapping them. I finally can't take it anymore and run at the cats, shooing them away. Now closer, I can smell the rats. I'm not sure if it's their mountain of shit underneath them, or the dead ones hanging like forgotten ornaments on some of the higher branches, some of them gutted, others just hanging limp and dried-out looking. They must have been hanging there for a while. Mom says rats need a lot of water. These ones don't have any water, that's for sure. The smell of their fear makes me take a step back. It's overwhelming. Worse than their shit. Worse than the freshly gutted ones, thanks to the patrolling cats that have learned to come like clockwork now for their daily feed. Dad said one time that rats seen during the day are the outcasts.

"They're so low on the totem pole their own kin have forced them to hunt for food during the day when the rest of their group is sleeping until nightfall, when normal rats hunt for their prey."

So the ones hanging on the Tree of Rats are the lowest of the low.

I hate the smell of a dead rat trapped in the walls. It's a stink that gets into your nose and no matter what you do, you can't get rid of it. It will follow you around all day, even when you leave the apartment and go to school. As much as Mom despises flies, she's learned how to find the exact spot where that dead and rotting rat is now by bringing a couple of green garbage flies into our place and releasing them.

"Don't kill the green ones!" she'll remind us, giving Ruth a certain look. But even Ruth knows these flies are special and will leave them alone until they do their job. They'll almost immediately go the part of the wall the rat's corpse is trapped behind. Then just sit there and make disgusting buzzing sounds. How did the dead rat get there in the first place? I've heard the squeaks and clawing of live rats behind the walls, heard them banging their heads on the inside of the toilet at night hoping to pop it open, but unable to get into our apartment thanks to the heavy brick we know to put on the lid each night. Sometimes you hear them fighting and it's so loud you'd think it was two small dogs in there. Rats are smart, too. I've watched them walk around a trap after one has been killed days before, as if they all know now to avoid it. Some of them even learn not to eat the poison the landlord sometimes will come and put around the flat, warning Mom that none of us kids should touch or eat it. Like we're all a bunch of idiots or like crawling babies who would put that crap into our mouths. Dad doesn't come over that often but when he does sometimes he pulls his gun like he might shoot one. I've heard him ask Mom right out, "Any rats around?"

I asked Mom one time why someone would want to make a Tree of Rats and she told me to stop talking nonsense.

"This is why everyone thinks you're a liar and a troublemaker."

Everyone thinks I'm a liar?

"If you tell people stuff like that you're just asking for trouble."

A liar and a troublemaker. Yup. That's me.

"I've had the same dream," says Ruth after Mom leaves the room.

I want to hug her but I'm afraid she'll push me away so I pretend not to hear her. I'm scared she'll be mad at herself for saying it out loud and then try and take it back. I want to ask her if the homeless guy was Grandpa. Is that what he did with the extra ones that he caught out of the kitchen floor? The ones nobody wanted to eat? Or maybe I made up that part up in my head, too.

Chapter Four

Nanny thinks my baby sister Hanna is possessed by the Devil. She gave everyone a fright when without any warning she suddenly fell to the ground, her eyes rolled to the back of her head and she started foaming like she had rabies or something. Then she started twitching and vibrating like she was being electrocuted. Dad happened to be with her when it happened and after yanking her up off the ground and carefully placing her still vibrating body into the back seat of his car, got her to the Children's Hospital in less than ten minutes. He must have done something funny to his back, though, 'cause the next day he couldn't walk. Hanna isn't so little anymore. At 13 she's the tallest girl in the family now, standing at five-foot-eight in her bare feet. Dad always calls her his beanpole. Nanny says what happened to Hanna is that she just threw a fit, something those possessed even just temporarily by the Devil sometimes do. That doesn't make any sense to me, though. I mean, why would the Devil try and possess Hanna? She's the sweetest and kindest person I know. She never has anything bad to say about anyone, always does her homework even though she knows that nobody is probably going to even look at it, and never tries to skip school or classes. She has a code she likes to follow, even though no one is forcing her to. It pissed me off when Nanny said it was the Devil taking over Hanna's body.

"Mom says it's something called 'epilepsy,'" I try explaining to Nanny.

"She's possessed," says Nanny. "But the good Lord can work miracles and cast out even the Evil One from those he's most attached to."

Hanna says her bed has been shaking sometimes in the middle of the night for a couple of years now, with explosions going off in her head. But she's been too afraid to tell anyone.

"Maybe I am the Devil," she says in a sad voice. "Maybe Nanny is right. I feel like I'm like that little girl Regan from *The Exorcist*."

Jesus Christ. Sometimes Nanny just makes me so mad.

"It proves that I really am dumb, too," says Hanna.

Mom took her to a special clinic for kids who have fits and Hanna says half of them in the room were having fits while she was waiting to see the doctor with Mom.

"A lot them are into sports, too," she says. "They were wearing helmets even while they waited."

Hanna says the drugs make her feel like a stoner and she keeps falling asleep in class now. She admitted she's afraid now that someone is going to stick her in an insane asylum after reading in some stupid history book that they used to do that years and years ago to people with epilepsy. It doesn't help that one of the doctors at the seizure clinic told her to not even think about ever driving a car.

"I hadn't thought about driving a car one day," says Hanna. "I didn't think I could ever even buy a car, never mind drive one. I'd be happy just to finish high school. So I feel dumb for feeling sad about something I never even knew I wanted."

Fucking doctors, anyway.

"When I saw those others kids at the clinic twitching on the floor and foaming like a dog with rabies," says Hanna, "it just…"

Hanna can't finish the thought but I know she's secretly worried she's now officially a retard. I want to tell her not to worry. That I'm the dumb one in the family. But for some reason I can't make the words come out. Mom told us all to stop calling it a "fit."

"It's a seizure," says Mom. "Your sister had a seizure. She has a brain disorder. It's not her fault."

I don't think anybody thought it was Hanna's fault. Even Nanny doesn't think it's Hanna's fault. She thinks it's the Devil's fault. I think Mom thinks it's Dad's fault; that it's somehow because of his family.

"That's crazy," says Dad. "Don't even go there. We both know who has the family of nutsos."

Hanna becomes famous for a while in our neighbourhood. The only thing that could have made her more famous was getting cancer. Or maybe losing half her fingers after ramming her hand into a meat grinder like that kid on Godin Avenue in Verdun did. Now that's a story. He was 15 or something and working at the corner store on weekends and after school. What I heard was that one day, without thinking while grinding up some hamburger meat, he just pushed his fingers into the grinder opening when the meat got a little stuck. And well, no one has been buying any meat from that corner store ever since. That kid is still famous. At least in Verdun. What an icky way to get famous.

"So your sister throws fits now, right?" says Lisa Melrose.

"Shut your stupid mouth," I tell her.

"What? I'm just asking a question. If she don't throw fits, fine!"

And Hanna worries that she's the retard? It doesn't take long for it to all die down, though, and soon enough, Hanna has to start reminding Mom about getting her the medication she needs about two weeks before she runs out of what she has.

"Mom, "says Hanna. "My pills. I'm going to need new ones again soon, okay?"

Sometimes Mom says sure, no problem. Other times she gets a little mad and crabby about it like Hanna has asked her to buy her something dumb and not worth the money.

"Christ on a stick," snaps Mom. "You'll get your medication! Money doesn't grow on trees around here, okay? You remember that!"

"Sorry," says Hanna. "I'm really sorry."

I felt bad for Hanna. When my ears used to ache so much when I was little that I'd sometimes stand on the railing of the back balcony on Rozel Street and think about whether the doctors would HAVE to give me something if I jumped, Mom would get mad if I complained too much, too. At first she'd be nice and even hold me on her lap, gently combing my hair with her fingers and saying she was sorry my ears were hurting and kiss my eyebrows. I'd hold back for as long as I could but finally those damn tears would force their way out and be running down my face, making Mom feel bad and not want to look at me anymore 'cause she couldn't help me. She'd stand up and say there wasn't a thing she could do and tell me to keep the warm water bottle on my own damn ear. I know Hanna already knows that money doesn't grow on trees, even if we had a tree in our backyard.

One time Hanna forgot to take her medication for four days and had one of her fits when Dad was visiting. Or that's what she said later when

Mom kept asking, "Why would you not take your damn pills? For four days? How could you forget?"

Dad had to scoop her up again and put her in the back seat of the car again and take her to the hospital. She seemed happy afterwards when, after he drove her back home and came into the apartment, he told all of us we had to be extra nice to her, and then patted her on the head before leaving again. Hanna's doctor told her not to tell anyone about the epilepsy, that she needs to keep it a secret and Mom agrees.

"People don't understand this disease," said the doctor, "and their ignorance makes them afraid. Just don't talk about it, okay?"

So Hanna stopped talking about it, even to us.

That means I never got to ask her about how scary it must have been to wake up and not remember anything that's happened to you for the last half hour, to realize you've wet yourself at school and everyone is staring at you. How come she didn't just stay in the house forever? She couldn't have felt safe anywhere ever again, right? But I couldn't ask. Hanna knew she had to keep it all a secret now.

A few years later, after we had all forgotten to wonder about Hanna's fits and even think about it anymore since we weren't allowed to speak of it, I heard her saying to Mom that she needs to write a letter to Margaret Atwood. The writer.

"Why do you want to write to Margaret Atwood?" asks Mom.

I want to ask how the hell Hanna even knows who the hell Margaret Atwood is but I don't want to be obvious about listening. I've read every single one of her books and each time I'm done one I can't believe she's a Canadian. Maybe she was adopted or moved here from the States when she was little? Annie has always said she's the writer who turned her off reading for good, though, after I begged her to read *The Edible Woman* and she did.

"Besides being boring as hell, I just couldn't get past that whole dumb stuff where she's writing about food like it's... like it's *people*. Plus, I didn't give a shit about what happened to Peter or Lucy so with nobody to root for, what's the point of reading it, right?"

I'm surprised to learn that Hanna has been reading Atwood's books, though, too. Never mind also planning to write her a damn letter.

"I want to ask her to stop using the word 'fit' in her stories," says Hanna.

Uh, what?

"What do you mean?" asks Mom. "You mean *the* Margaret Atwood? The writer?"

If there's one way to get our mother's attention it's to tell her you have plans to confront someone who is important or has any kind of power. Of course, she knows who Margaret Atwood is.

"I've read two of her books now where she uses that word," says Hanna. "Where she has characters 'throwing fits.' I just want to let her know how mean that is. And just wrong."

I try to remember now if I have ever used the word "fit." Damn. I know I have but I forget why it's bad and I'm afraid to ask Hanna. I don't want her to think I'm mean or a dumb ass like that goddamn Margaret Atwood is. Now I'm waiting to see Mom's reaction. On the one hand she could instantly become upset and act like Hanna's a wasteful idiot, wanting to spend money on a stamp to write a letter of complaint to a writer. On the other, Mom is big on action and using your voice when any kind of injustice has been committed. More than once she's announced something about the "fallacy of agency being the most important deception that all of us tell ourselves." Whatever the Christ that means. I think she stole that from one of the dykes at McGill. There's also that idea about Hanna's fits needing to be kept a big secret, too. Shit, I mean Hanna's "epilepsy." I'm sure Hanna is relieved when Mom seems to decide that Hanna is being brave for confronting someone important.

Mom hunts around in her bedroom for a minute and then comes out with a stamp and envelope for Hanna.

She slowly, in a shy voice, reads her letter out loud to us. She explains to Margaret Atwood that on behalf of all epileptics, they prefer to use the word "seizure" instead of the word "fit."

Hanna writes the best letter I've ever read anywhere. We made her read one part out loud twice:

"When you have the protagonist using that word in regards to another person in the story it completely legitimizes the use of a word that is so hurtful and nasty to those of us who have to deal with the fallout each and every day."

Well, fuck me. And Hanna actually worries about maybe being a retard? Or dumb in any way at all? She's writing to a big shot like Ms. Margaret Atwood and calling her out on her shit like that? Damn. "Hanna? You know this means you're super smart and brave, right?" I say, and I really mean it. Hanna acts all shy and embarrassed, like she doesn't know what to do with her hands now.

I'm not sure which of us were more shocked and impressed when Hanna actually got a letter back a few weeks later from Margaret Atwood herself. Hanna reads it out loud.

Dear Hanna Dobson,

Thank you for your letter and your kind words. I am glad you've enjoyed my writing. Regarding the use of "epileptic fit," you're confusing me, the writer, with the characters in my books. I am not Alfred or Elaine and I've never had any luck dictating what my characters should think or how they should behave. They are different people; they are not me. They are people whose understanding of the world is imperfect and limited, like most of the people you see around me. In a perfect world they might say "seizure" instead of "epileptic fit" but the world's not perfect—one of the reasons I write.

Sincerely, Margaret Atwood.

Holy. Shit. She's not in charge of her characters? They get to walk on the page and say or do anything they want? She doesn't make them behave or do what she wants? Is that how it works for writers? An asshole just shows up in their head one day and the writer puts them in a book? Lets them roam around all free and crazy, saying anything they want to? Help make them famous even if they're assholes? Well, isn't that just great.

"I should rip this up," says Hanna, and Mom and I both say, "No!" at the same time.

I don't remember if we ever talked about Hanna's epilepsy again but I know it was that day I finally learned to stop saying the word "fit" forever.

All of us girls always have a book in front of us and ever since our sister Ruth started working at the People's Library in the Point we all have tons to read now all the time. Even new books, now that Ruth has taught me how to take books out of real libraries, so that's not scary anymore, either. The books from the People's Library in the Point sometimes smell a little funny, but the ones in the public library near my school might sometimes look old but they don't smell like anything.

"Now if there's anything you want to learn about, anything at all, you don't have to ask anybody nothing," explained Ruth. "And you don't have to listen to their lies. You can just look it up yourself. At the library."

I'm shocked when I realize I can even read newspapers and magazines at the library for free, too. No more having to believe someone when they say they read it in the paper, or a book. If it sounds like bullshit to me, I can look it up and see for myself. Or if someone isn't telling me something, I can find out about that, too. I read all about Uncle Luther being the Handsome Smiling Bank Robber in the Montreal *Gazette* at the library. The tellers all liked him, even though he was robbing them, on account of how good-looking he is and how he would always smile so friendly-like, even as he pointed a gun at them. It was exciting to read a newspaper article about how he finally got caught by a helicopter, and on St. Catherine Street, right downtown. So yeah, no one can tell me lies anymore, or keep stuff secret. I can find out anything I pretty much want to now, thanks to the library. The guy at the desk in charge of the place, his name is Andrew, is pretty good about answering all of my questions, too. Never acts like I'm an idiot for wondering about it, either. He just calmly brings me over to the wooden boxes and shows me how to look stuff up.

"The only stupid thing would be not asking a question when you so easily can," said Andrew. "That's why I'm here."

After dropping out of high school for a couple of years in grade 9 and then finally going back this year, I admit I have a new attitude towards education. I know that sounds all fake and like suck-up bullshit but it's really true. I know I can't tell teachers to fuck off anymore, no matter how much they're trying to make me look dumb by asking me to list all the provinces and capital cities of Canada in front of the whole class. I mean, come on. Who really knows that shit, right? I mean other than maybe Annie, of course. And maybe my dad. And my sisters. And our mom. But still. Why ask the one person in the fucking room who you know doesn't have the answer when there's a whole row of keeners waving their arms around like they're gonna stroke out on the spot if you don't call on them? I also know now that I can't get any job except for babysitting if I don't finish high school. So now I'm in the hairdressing program at LaSalle High School.

No, for real. I'm in a hairdressing program. It means I get to be a hairdresser in two years after I graduate from high school. Ya-fucking-hoo. A high school graduate *and* a hairdresser, all in one shot. Hairdressing class is every single day, for most of the morning. I admit it's not as easy as I thought it would be. We aren't just cutting hair all day and then sweeping it up. Nope. And each day is different. Some days? You gotta make sure you don't kill nobody. For real.

Like yesterday. As soon as the water hit her scalp, I watched in horror as Mrs. Bounds' hair, still tightly wound in the perm rollers, falls into the sink. Each curler rod makes a light clink as it drops off her head and clatters into the sink, sounding like pennies dropping onto the floor. Except with pennies, you can just pick them up and put them back in your pocket. I can't put Mrs. Bounds' hair back on.

Mrs. Bernie, the hairdressing teacher, suddenly appears beside me. I wonder what tipped her off that there was a problem—the fact that I had stopped breathing and moving, or that Mrs. Bounds' hair isn't where it was supposed to be.

"Did you put the neutralizer on?" she asks calmly. I know she's just trying to buy some time. If I had already put the neutralizer on, we both know Mrs. Bounds' hair would still be on her head and not in the sink.

"The timer," Mrs. Bernie says. "When did it go off?"

Ah. The timer. That was pretty much all Mrs. Bernie had talked about the week before during our section on Hair Processing.

"As soon as a chemical makes contact with someone's hair, the timer comes out," she had told us over and over again. I used to think she was so anal. Now I know she was so right. I try to decide which is worse: that I never set the timer? Or that I ignored it when it went off? Mrs. Bernie is looking at me. Her face is demanding an answer. I quickly make a decision.

"I forgot to set it, and… I just lost track of time," I say, deciding to go with the truth.

I hadn't known there was so much science to this hairdressing stuff. With all the business about chemicals and timers, and even an anatomy class where we learned about the lungs, you'd think we were training to become freaking surgeons, instead of just cutting people's hair. When I put "the lung" as an answer on a test one time, the teacher put a large red x through the word "lung," then wrote next to it, "We have two lungs. Lung is plural in this context." What the fuck is with teachers that can't just be clear and say it straight up. I mean, I know they have to be fancy and all that but she could have written: "Lung is plural. 'Cause you got two." My sisters made fun of me for days after I told them about that. About me thinking she should have said "plural, 'cause you got two of them." "Oh, look at you," said Ruth. "Being all fancy with the plurals and lungs and stuff."

I wanted to punch her right in the neck.

My sisters knew why I was stuck at LaSalle Public High School, taking bobo classes and learning how to cut hair. I hadn't even enrolled in the program to become a hairdresser. It was just my ticket through high school. I had dropped out because since grade seven my report cards had basically been long lists of Fs. Once I made the decision to go back to school, since I didn't have the marks to get into nursing like my sister Annie, the only way I could graduate was by taking a trade. And I didn't want to learn how to fix cars. What the hell did I know or care about cars?

I remember my meeting with the school's guidance counsellor.

"You could go into the auto trades program," he says, sliding some information packets towards me. Has he ever actually looked at these things? The guy in the picture is smiling while he jabs a wrench into the front of a car, a bunch of hoses and pipes that looks like a maze from some kid's activity book. Except the maze doesn't look very fun—there's black stuff oozing out of one of the pipes and onto the smiling guy's hands. He looks happy to have his hands covered in something that looks like a pile of liquid dog shit you might see in the park.

"Girls can be anything today!" says the guidance counsellor. He seems to genuinely believe that offering me the chance to be a grease monkey or a hairdresser for the rest of my life is some kind of proof of us coming a long way, baby. The new me knows not to tell him to fuck off or make a bunch of snarky remarks about his job, and ask what does a girl need to do these days to get to sit behind a desk and tell students they can be anything they want. Well, as long as they want to be A or B, of course.

Going into hairdressing wasn't really a choice. It was only through the process of elimination that I was now standing beside Mrs. Bounds, her bald head to my right, and all of her hair to my left. I swear, only an old person would let a bunch of students screw around with their hair just to save a few bucks. They still have to pay the school for the chemicals and then usually give us a tip as well. So it's not as if it's free.

I glance between the hair-filled sink and Mrs. Bounds' barren scalp, wondering if this situation is possibly fixable. Screwing up someone's bangs is fixable—like spilling a drink on their living room rug. An apology and a quick cleanup, and you hardly notice the damage. But melting someone's hair off? That's like burning their house down. All you can do is stare at the ashes.

Mrs. Bernie starts rinsing what remains of Mrs. Bounds' hair and for the first time I notice the angry red splotches that have started to appear at her hairline. Mrs. Bounds is still humming pleasantly with her eyes closed, oblivious to the fact that her weekly trim has turned into an accidental shave. She's used to having the teacher hover and oversee our work and has no clue yet about the train wreck unfolding all around her.

"Grab a garbage bag," Mrs. Bernie instructs, starting to smear a heavy cream along Mrs. Bounds' hairline. "You need to get rid of those," she adds quietly, motioning towards the dead soldiers in the sink. I know what she's thinking. When Mrs. Bounds snaps out of her trance and realizes something's up, seeing her hair in a sad pileup in the sink probably isn't the best way to break the news to her. I wonder what we'll say.

"Your scalp was shot down over the Sea of Japan… there were no survivors."

I quickly stuff the rollers into the garbage bag. Normally touching huge clumps of someone's hair would ick me out. It's bad enough when it's attached to their head, but pulling it out of the sink still attached to rollers feels like tossing a hand with a ring still attached. I get busy, knowing I need to bury the evidence as quickly as possible. I admit it. I was already thinking ahead to later that day. How my sisters were going to react when I told them the story of Old Lady Hair, looking like a chewed-up sweater, sitting in the deep sink.

Once the bag is out of sight Mrs. Bernie clears her throat. "Mrs. Bounds? I have good news and bad news."

Mrs. Bounds immediately knows something is up and starts reaching for her hair. Or at least, where she thinks her hair is. Where her hair should be.

"Yes, that's the bad news," Mrs. Bernie says. "Sometimes my students can be a little... overly ambitious," she smiles. "I know it's maybe a little shorter than you had hoped for, but the good news is that it's only hair and will grow back, of course, and the rest of your visits until the end of this school year are on the house!"

I'm amazed when the old doll seems to buy into it. Or at least be thinking it over. Mrs. Bernie is a freaking master. She's holding up a mirror, trying to Jedi mind-control the old biddy with a mental push.

"See? You still have enough on top for some real lift there and now you'll just have to give it a quick rub after a shower and presto, for the next six weeks or so you've got a real easy wash-and-wear style!"

I'm shocked when I notice that Mrs. Bounds looks pleased, as if this is actually a good trade-off. Have a student burn off every strand of your hair within an inch and a half of your scalp and in exchange, even more opportunities in the future for giving students a shot at making you look like Mr. Bounds instead of Mrs. Bounds. Yup, offer something for free, and watch the lineup form to the left. I'm gonna start offering free kicks to the ass.

"Come with me, please," says Mrs. Bernie. She doesn't even bother to look to see if I'm following. She knows I want to get as far away from the crime scene as quickly as possible.

"Tell me, what have you learned from this?" she asks, once we're safely out of earshot of the burnt and crispy looking baldy mutant over by the sinks. I know not to say, "That I'm right about hairdressing. That it fucking sucks."

Instead, I know to look away and wait. When a teacher asks you a question like that, they're usually just waiting for you to shut up long enough so they can tell you, in great detail, all about what you haven't learned. And what you should have. And why you should. And why you're a complete fuck-up for not having done so already.

So I wait.

I stare at my shoes and vow not to react, no matter what Mrs. Bernie says next. I need to graduate. I have to graduate. I no longer allow myself the luxury of telling teachers to go fuck themselves.

"Kathy, please look at me."

I look up without thinking. Mrs. Bernie is leaning against her desk, her arms crossed, her face doesn't look angry. She looks… concerned.

"Share your thought process with me," she says. "We'll never figure out what went wrong if we don't reverse-engineer it, right now, while the memories are still fresh. Walk me through the whole procedure. Let's start with her sitting down. She's got her cape on. Her hair is all rolled up. The rods are set. Now think. What did you do next?"

What the fuck? I've been in Mrs. Bernie's class for about two months now and I keep waiting for her eyes to roll to the back of her head and the fangs to come out. Or for her to lose it when one of us makes asshole mistakes. Like the one I just did. A really big asshole mistake. I can't figure her out. What's she up to?

Although I'm in the hairdressing program full-time, I'm officially a grade 11 student at LaSalle Public School. Thanks to being in one of the trades, though, my "academic" schedule includes only three other subjects: English, French and history. It means I get to hang out in hairdressing most of the time and attend the other classes only twice a week. It's like I've won the Lucky Student Lottery, though, as I actually don't hate my other teachers, either. I mean, I hate French class of, course. Is there anything worse than having to force yourself to sound like an idiot and babble away, all in an attempt to prove to the French teacher that you're at least trying? But the good thing is that no one else in the bobo French class I'm in sounds any better. I think I'm in the dumb-ass class for history, too. If I thought making newborn baby sounds in French class was boring, my history class could be used as a form of torture. I'm not sure if it's the teacher or the material. Or both. But I have to bite my bottom lip and dig my nails into my palms sometimes, just to stay awake. I'm finally learning that as long as a teacher thinks you respect them, and their boring shit, they'll pretty much leave you alone. And if you can make them believe that, unlike the rest of the students who are ready to explode out of their classroom the instant the bell goes, you actually wish their class could go an extra ten minutes, well… okay, nobody would buy that. Not even the dumbest of the dumb teachers. Like Mrs. Hurran. And seriously? She's not only the biggest asshole I've ever had as a teacher, she's also the most boring. And coming from me that says a lot.

"If we've learned anything as a society," declares Mrs. Hurran, "it's that history will repeat itself." She delivers that line so slowly, it's obvious that it's one of her favourites. You just know she says that one every single year and in the exact same voice. The Emmas and Peggys and Debras in the room all quickly write it down in their notebooks, nodding their heads at the teacher's brilliance. The old me would have made sure my yawn could be heard across the room. I might have even loudly asked one of the ass-crack lickers if they were for real. Instead, I force myself to smile at Mrs. Hurran, hoping my face somehow conveys how profound and deep I consider the notion that history repeats itself. Yawn.

"War is a reoccurring theme throughout history, and our reaction in times of…" I tune her out. I almost wish she'd tell her story again about needing surgery a couple of years ago to get herself peeing straight again. Teachers are so used to their students being a captive audience, I think they start thinking their shit is actually interesting. They think those rows and rows of faces all staring at them are actually listening, instead of in a fucking coma. People must hate teachers at parties.

My favourite class is English, which shocks the shit out of me. I've always thought having an "English" class when you're already well, English, kind of stupid. Mr. Thomas, the English teacher, has what I eventually learn is a Caribbean accent, and it sounds so soft and musical, I would happily listen to him recite the school cafeteria menu. It's so strange to hear that soft, low voice coming out of such a tall and strong-looking man. When he smiles, he really owns it. He always says that we need to write about what we know but the problem is I don't know anything.

"This means drawing from the deep well of your own lives and lived experiences," he says to the class.

Hell, stuff better start happening to me soon. What's really weird, though, is that he seems to think I'm not dumb.

"Kathy, your essay about your grandmother was deeply moving and showed some incredible insight into our culture's impatience with the elderly. Perhaps even our own fear of death and becoming vulnerable and dependent on the goodwill of others."

What? I wrote some "insights"? Me? I assumed he'd mixed my paper up with someone else's in class who had written about their grandmother too, but I didn't feel the need to set him straight. I could feel my face growing red under his praise. The funny thing about Mr. Thomas, though, is that on the one hand he'll tell you how "creative and interesting and compelling your prose is," then hand you back your paper with all kinds of comments scrawled between the lines and in the margins, detailing what exactly you fucked up on.

"Content is more critically important than the ladders we use to get there," he'll say. I have no clue what the hell that means, of course, but since he's smiling at me with his beautiful white teeth and nodding his head, I figure it's okay, despite the tiny attacks all over the page. The main problem is that since I've somehow managed to trick him into thinking I'm smart or something, sometimes Mr. Thomas will call on me to answer a question in class and I have no clue what in hell he's talking about.

"Kathy," he's looking at me from the front of the room. "Would you please start us off on a positive note this morning and write one or two examples of the Parts of Speech on the board, please?"

He nods and holds out a piece of chalk. I have no choice. I don't know what I'm going to do when I get there—the front of the room, the whole class watching—but I know it isn't going to include me writing a part of some speech on the blackboard. I don't even know how to ask for further instructions or explanation of what he's actually asking me to do. I'm at ground zero when it comes to this kind of shit but for some reason this teacher thinks I not only know it, but that I'm ready to show it off to the rest of the class. I want to run out of the room but that seems too disrespectful to the first high school teacher I've ever really wanted to impress. Gun to my head, though, I can't think of any speech, ever. Have I ever even heard a speech before? I mean, on purpose? Well, unless the speech my mom gave in front of the riot squad a few years back, the one that she made up on the spot counts. She even gave it a title, like a poem.

"Is it okay if I read the 'Poor People's Prayer'?" said Mom to the guy standing closest to her. I wasn't sure he had even heard her, what with his tight-fitting thick helmet that even had a shield in front of it, like my mom might spit or something when she talks.

I realize Mr. Thomas is waiting for me.

"I don't feel so good," I say when I reach the front of the room. I do a vague rubbing of my lower stomach, hoping to convey an air of serious sickness impending. I know it's the lamest play ever, but I'm desperate. Mr. Thomas frowns.

"Would you like a few minutes?" He asks. Then says, "Go ahead."

After rummaging through his desk for a second, he hands me a hall pass. I keep my head down as I leave the room. Damn, damn, damn. Why can't I be smart? Why can't I be the person he thinks I am? Why don't I know any speeches? How the hell do other kids know speeches? I mean, my mother is the only person I know who gives speeches, but they aren't in any books. How come other kids seem to somehow know speeches by famous people? What the hell is wrong with me? Mr. Thomas probably hates me now. I wonder if it's too late now to brag to Ruth that she's not the only writer in our family anymore. I probably shouldn't. I'd just be cursing myself for borrowing happiness from the future like Nanny always says.

When our French teacher handed out the class textbooks, I had to bite back all of the smart-ass comments. But my god, I'm not kidding, it's a fucking comic book! A thick one, yes, and it's in French. But it's a damn picture book! I quickly flip through the pages and try not to laugh out loud. There are trucks and city workers and traffic lights and near the end of the story, an accident involving a whole lot of trucks on fire. "Un feu!" screams one of the tiny dialogue bubbles. Oh fuck. A French comic book. A boring French comic book. About trucks. You couldn't make this shit up. I can't wait to make my sister Annie laugh about it later.

"No fucking way!" she says after I hand her my comic book. "Do French people really find this shit interesting?" she asks as she quickly flips through the pages.

"Look at how they make explosion sounds in French," she says, pointing to the page with two huge trucks on fire after colliding with each other.

"Well, at least you'll know how to make sense to any French cops who might show up after you've rammed one huge motherfucking truck with another," she says.

I'm glad that she isn't making fun of me, an 18-year-old former high-school dropout now sitting in a baby French class, sounding like a complete and utter moron every time I have to pretend I'm trying my best while fumbling through the class textbook for the teacher. At least the teacher seems like a nice guy. He never laughs or rolls his eyes. He never puts anyone on the spot, and after forcing you to sound something out, never mocks you by mimicking you like my last French teacher at Westmount High used to like to do. It was so satisfying when I finally told him, in plain English, to go fuck himself and tossed the top of his desk. Asshole. This guy, though, seems just sad when I don't know how to say something right. His eyes seem to say, "It's okay, really. Just try your best."

The teachers at LaSalle High don't seem to know anything about my past experiences with teachers, thank god. I know they'd hate me if they did. With these teachers I have a chance to start over. Be a different person. Someone who isn't angry all the time. Someone who doesn't hate everyone just because they have socks and real jeans and stuff that fits and doesn't look like it came from the clothing room of the church basement. Every morning, just before I go into the school, I remind myself not to tell anyone to go fuck themselves. And to always just admit it when I don't know. Teachers seem to like that. Saves them the trouble of having to call you a dumb ass themselves.

Except for English class. Somehow I've fallen into the stupid trap of pretending I'm a smart student. Mr. Thomas will eventually learn the truth about me, I guess, but until then, I'm enjoying having him assume I know so much more than I do. Well, assuming I know anything at all. Anything that matters. In a classroom. To a teacher.

"You're a good writer, maybe even great," he says to me one day. I forget to breathe and want to sit down. "Yeah?" I say.

Then I spend the next two weeks reliving the most exciting moment of my life, followed by my most embarrassing. Why couldn't I have thought of something less stupid to say than "Yeah?" Christ on a stick.

"Yes, you are," he said in response.

He doesn't just tell us to write in complete sentences. He speaks in complete sentences. Everything he says sounds more happy and true and important because of his accent. Who could sound so pretty and lie at the same time? I wanted to beg for details but he caught me off guard. On my long list of quick replies to teachers' questions or comments about my work, I had nothing for a moment like this.

"You should go to college. Have you thought about what you might take?"

I had to force myself to look all casual. Like having a conversation with one of my teachers about me one day going to college was as normal as not going to school naked.

"What do ya mean?" I ask. Then realize I made it all sound like one extra-long word.

"Whatdoyamean?"

Mr. Thomas grins. Then says it again.

"College. You should think about it."

Sure, that and going to the fucking moon. Or China. Right. There's also that fine line with some Point people when it comes to education. A high school certificate is pretty rare so it's worthy of celebration and even proof that you come from a good and decent family, giving your parents major bragging rights. But college or university? That's just showing off and putting on airs. But Mr. Thomas suggesting I think about college is like telling me that if I swallow a fly or wave my pencil in the air like a wand I could suddenly become a superhero. Then again,

73

if someone had told me I'd one day fall in love with a tall, skinny black guy with a pretty voice and white Chiclet teeth, I'd have told them to go fuck themselves. Skinny guys with pretty voices don't do so well in my neighbourhood. Black people are invisible. Well, usually. Mr. Thomas wouldn't be invisible. He'd probably get the shit kicked out of him.

When some of the school's toughest kids gather together in their spot in a corner of the cafeteria, I'm always surprised by how afraid the teachers all seem. These kids aren't the kind of tough that would suddenly stab you in the eye with a fork for looking at them funny, or wait for you in the school's parking lot to bounce your face off the windshield of your own car. They aren't from the Point, Little Burgundy or Verdun. No, these kids are mostly all mouth and maybe some shoving if you get in their way. But the teachers all give them a wide berth. I mostly ignore them and because they can tell I'm too old to be in grade 11 but not old enough to be a teacher, they pretend not to see me. They seem to sense my lack of fear. It's not that I underestimate them. I don't. I know they'd kick the shit out of anyone who'd offer up too much mouth back or any serious resistance. But I also know, in a way I can't explain even to myself, that they don't underestimate me, either. Once in a while they'll corner some white kid to harass and the whole cafeteria will go quiet while everyone watches. They snatched a lunch bag from a grade seven and had started to laugh and toss it back and forth when suddenly Mr. Thomas was standing between them, glaring at the kid holding the crushed bag with his arm raised, just about to toss it across the room.

"How dare you."

At first I didn't even know it was Mr. Thomas. I looked around to see who had said it, then looked back and realized it was Mr. Thomas. I mean, it kind of looked like him and all but it was the voice. The pretty voice was gone. The look of rage on his face was so fierce the entire cafeteria froze. The kid who had just been trying to catch his crumpled lunch bag back looked down at his feet. Even he didn't want… this.

"Are we animals now?" growled Mr. Thomas. "Animals prowling among the weak and imposing our brute strength? Playing cruel games with the vulnerable?"

Shit. Now there was a speech for the next time.

Everyone seemed to know that these were questions that didn't expect or demand an answer. I silently moved to the rear of Mr. Thomas. His rage was fueling his fearlessness in a way I knew could get him hurt. No teacher ever talked to these kids like that. Mr. Thomas was going to get his ass kicked. Or at least a stray half-empty Coke can off the back of his unprotected head. It's amazing how much happened in the next fraction of a second. I could hear them all thinking. Going back and forth between the possibilities. And then finally.

"Aw, fuck it," said the kid holding the ruined lunch then tossed it back at the grade seven. Everyone seemed to take a deep breath at the same time. People started to move, pushing back chairs, sipping last bits of their Coke tins. Mr. Thomas looked smaller. I turned around and left.

Chapter Five

SOMETIMES I CAN'T BELIEVE I have a boyfriend. And he's not from the Point, either. No, Jack is like one of those boyfriends on TV. He brushes his teeth every day and not just before going to the dentist or something fancy, either. He also takes a shower every single day whether he needs it or not, and never swears. Ever. He's tall and handsome and even smells good. I met him through my sister Julia's boyfriend Matt. They're like best friends. Julia just told me one day that Matt's friend, Jack, had seen me standing with her at the bus stop one day and wanted to meet me.

"Is he cute?" I asked Julia, though I'm really just trying to distract her so she won't be able to tell how excited I am.

"Sure," says Julia. "He's really tall. Even taller than Matt."

After that first date we started seeing each other every single day. When a couple of the other students from my hairdressing class saw him waiting outside the door, one of them snorted and said, "What is that loser doing out there?"

Loser? What?

"Do you mean Jack?" I said. "He's waiting for *me*."

The girl instantly backed down.

"Oh, sorry about that! I didn't mean anything!"

Jealous bitch. Wonder how she knew his name, though?

When I told Jack a few months after we'd been dating that I have to find a part-time job that pays me better than babysitting because my mom expects me to pay her some room and board if I want to go to college, 'cause "no one gets a free ride around here!" he looks shocked. I immediately try to backpedal a bit. I'm not sure when the exact moment arrived when I realized my mother doesn't like me very much, but I do remember how hard I've always worked at making sure no one else will ever figure it out. I mean, what would people think of me if they knew my own mother doesn't love me? It's embarrassing. I start to tell Jack that

I don't blame her, it's not like she can afford to support any of us at home going off to college or university, but he interrupts me to say we should look for a place together.

"We're together most of the time now, anyway," he says.

He's right. We do spend all of our free time together now. He helps me a lot with school. I'm almost finished now and know I never would have done half as well if he hadn't been helping me all the time. He makes me read from my French book almost every day after school and gently corrects my pronunciation, never laughing or cracking any jokes about how bad I sound. I wonder how we can afford it, though. He's a student, too. He's in psychology at McGill University. But his parents support him. They have serious jobs and lots of money.

He brings me to see the basement apartment he thinks we can move into together in LaSalle and says it's not far from downtown and is super close to McGill and Dawson College. I wonder what would bug my mother more: me going to college, or me living in sin with my boyfriend? Jack warns me that the kitchen is real small.

"But it has a working fridge and stove."

Okay, like I'll ever use them. But still, I couldn't see a downside. I'd be moving from my mom's crowded city-housing apartment with the tiny bathroom you have to stand in line for each morning, to living with Jack. Just Jack. No more sleeping on a bunk bed. No more sharing or anyone borrowing my socks or underwear. Yup.

"I don't know how to cook anything anyway," I say to Jack. He looks at me for a second, then throws his head back and laughs. I'm not sure why that's so funny but I laugh along with him.

"I'll teach you," he says with a huge grin.

How fucking lucky am I? Of course, I don't really give two shits about learning how to cook. I want to ask why people who know how to cook always assume that those of us who don't are somehow dying to learn. Nothing I eat really needs more than a toaster or, at most, a toaster oven. I know how to make fish. Fish sticks are about as fancy as I get. The first time I saw what Annie explained to me is a "salad spinner" I couldn't believe the stupid shit that rich people find to waste their money on. One time I had dinner at Jack's parents' place and they served weird crap like "sprouts" and "avocado." I mean, seriously, who buys and eats that stuff on purpose? The more weird and strange the food is, the fancier it seems to rich people. If one more person offers me a recipe for something I might scream. I need to stop saying I don't like to cook. It seems like it's code for "give me a million recipes, please."

The first time I made a meal for Jack, after he had already made me tons of dinners, I had to ask my older sisters what I could make to go with the fish sticks.

"What do normal people eat?" I asked Annie and Ruth.

Even I knew that I couldn't just give him a pile of fish sticks and nothing else, no matter how many were on the plate. Maybe some bread and real butter? Would that be enough?

"What about some BBQ chips with them?" said Annie. But I had already thought about that and worried it would look like I was mixing healthy with unhealthy stuff. And Jack seemed like the healthy-eating kind.

"What about some mashed potatoes?" said Ruth.

Hmmm. Mashed potatoes? I knew it would make her fucking year but I had no choice, I had to ask.

"Okay. How do you make mashed potatoes?"

To her credit, Ruth only made me wait a few seconds as she licked her lips, then tried real hard not to crack her knuckles in joy right in front of me before speaking.

"You just boil them in a huge pot of water for a while until they get soft, then add some butter and milk," said Ruth. Then she took a breath. "After a while, once some disgusting looking white foam rises to the top of the water, you stick a fork in them when you think they're ready and if the fork slips in easy, they're done!"

When Ruth says shit like this I know she's just reminding us that she didn't grow up with the rest of us girls. Unlike us, with Mom on welfare in the Point, Ruth got to grow up with Nanny like an only child, with Popsicles after praising the Lord and singing shitty hymns at church every Sunday. Ruth didn't have to share her underwear or socks and got to eat all kinds of fancy foods we didn't even know existed, including real hot-dog buns for her hot dogs, until we went to Camp

Amy Molson while our mother worked in the kitchen. At camp all of our hot dogs came in buns, no matter how many we ate. I hate it when Ruth shows off like this. She knows what pots to use, how to use them, and likes food I think is icky. Potatoes are supposed to be brown and crispy French fries, not a pale and soft heap of white crap.

"What about a salad?" said Annie. "I bet that's what people like Jack love to eat. You could chop up a tomato and add some onions and a cucumber to it. You know, with some lettuce. Then just put some mayonnaise on it like Nanny does when she makes a nice salad on Sundays!"

Does anyone really like that shit? A cucumber? It tastes like grass, and not the good kind of grass. And what if Annie was wrong? Maybe Jack hates salad and like me, doesn't think it's real food.

"Cheese chunks?" says Ruth. "Isn't that what rich people do when they want to be fancy? You know, maybe with some Ritz crackers or something?"

Hmmmm. This has potential.

"I don't want to look all fake and show-off-y, though," I say, but I admit I'm warming up to the idea and just want to try it on for size. I also want them to talk me into it. Then if Jack looks embarrassed for me, or something, I can just say my sisters put me up to it.

Ruth instructs us that cheese and crackers always need to have their own serving plates. Fucking Jesus Christ. This is why I hate fucking cooking or trying to feed someone. Can't we just shove a goddamn sandwich down our throats and be done? This is getting way too complicated.

"Well, what about just a bologna and cheese sandwich then?"

Hell, even I know how to slap a slice of bologna and cheese on some bread and cut it into two nice, perfect triangles. I can make that look pretty good, actually. I could even go all out and toast it.

"You know it's made with pigs' asses and cows' tails, right?" says Ruth.

Oh Christ, now I've made her day. She thinks she knows Something Important that I don't.

"Eeew!" says Annie. "That's not true and you know it!"

Like me, Annie is probably thinking about all of those tightly rolled slices of bologna around a French fry that we've eaten over the years.

"It's the truth!" insists Ruth. "My science teacher said it's made up of all the rejected and leftover parts of farm animals. And Nanny grew up on a farm in Gaspé and she says everyone down there knows it. Bologna is called a poor person's steak for a reason! It's why Nanny won't touch it. She knows!"

Then why does Nanny buy bologna that isn't even sliced? It's like a huge pink log. Like a pig already missing its head, feet and tail.

"That way I can make it as thick or as thin as I like," says Nanny. She's served me plenty of thick slices of fried pig, I mean bologna, over the years. That's just Ruth putting on airs again.

"Your science teacher is just messing with you, Ruth."

I know this will send her into a complete frenzy and it does.

"As Nanny herself will tell you, God doesn't reject any part of any animal. Unless we're talking about the Jewish God, and he says not to eat any animals with a split hoof, which means goats are out but bologna is in. The hoof of a bologna is split-free."

Annie starts to laugh and I know I've won.

"Fine," says Ruth and stands up. "Figure out your meal stuff with Jack on your own, then."

Oops. I hadn't meant to piss her off that much.

Jesus, why does it matter if I cook something myself, with my own two hands, anyway? Why can't I just order some KFC?

"Oh, guys see that as super important," explains Annie. "It shows that you care enough to put in the effort."

Put in the effort? Do guys have any idea how much effort goes into making sure your makeup and hair are just right? How much time is spent on picking out which shirt looks best with your jeans? How much time is spent on practicing certain reactions, depending on what he says or does? I still don't even understand what Jack is talking about half the time, anyway. Sometimes he talks about some guy, with a weird name, something like "Tie Ching," and I can tell he's super impressed with him. I'm hoping I never have to actually meet him or anything 'cause I know I won't understand a word he says. With a name like that, he probably has a funny accent, too. Jack recently said something about the further you go, the less you know, and "at the end of your journey you will discover that you have never moved at all." Like, what the fuck?

When I pretended to be super impressed, Jack quickly told me it wasn't his line, but a quote.

"That's pure *I Ching*," said Jack.

Maybe Tie is simple in the head or something? And what kind of a last name is that, anyway? I wonder if he can cook. Seriously, though, why do guys need you to cook for them anyway, on top of everything else?

And Holy Christ, I never knew how loud my peeing was until the first time I had to go after we moved into our apartment and while Jack waited on the other side of the door asking me what was taking so long, I had to run the tap in the bathroom sink to muffle the sound. I knew then I'd never be able to take a shit in peace ever again. Or at least not at home. I just hold it in and wait until I'm at school or work. If I ever feel comfortable enough that I'll be taking a shit while Jack's around I figure it'll be time to leave. The first night in our apartment I realize he's used to sleeping in the dark.

"Uh, can we leave a light on, okay?"

Jack thinks it's funny that a girl from the Point is afraid of the dark.

"This is not only a nice neighbourhood," says Jack, "you've got me. You're completely safe, babe."

Why do I love it when he calls me "babe"? It's so lame. But I'm not afraid of anyone breaking in. Let them try.

"I just don't like the dark," I say to Jack. I know not to tell him that even if someone did break in, guys like him don't actually know how to fight. Guys like him start off by asking way too many questions, like they think it's still negotiable and if the right words are said they can calm everything down. Next, once they realize that they're going to be forced to engage, they toss insults out like that might somehow wound the other guy so badly, he'll rethink his life choices and simply pick up his baseball bat and go home. Then finally, they'll spar and think it's going to be some wrestling match until the other guy finally admits defeats and says, "Whoa, you're so much stronger than I expected. I give!" Point guys just beat the shit out of each other until someone stops moving. It's like my dad always says, two wrongs make a good fight.

The problem with Jack is that he's all into this weird "Rosicrucian" crap that to be honest sounds a lot like Nanny's church to me, but without the fancy building filled with wooden pews, and the singing of hymns during weekly gatherings each Sunday. You think I'd know to shut up about some stuff, right? Jack is deeply offended by the comparison.

"The Rosicrucian tradition is part of an ancient and secret brotherhood!"

I know not to say out loud how creepy that sounds to me. Maybe even worse than Nanny's church. Plus, her church is pretty old as shit, too.

"The Rosicrucian manifesto exists to advance the arts and sciences. It's a fellowship that aspires to prepare us to develop our minds in a spirit of unselfish service to others."

Okay, that stupid shit sounds exactly like the kind of sermon I heard Nanny's preacher give only about a million times when I was little.

"This isn't about religion," says Jack. "This is about spirituality."

Why do people think saying they're only "spiritual" and not "religious" makes them sound any less stupid? But Jack's not done.

"As Teilhard de Chardin himself has said, we are not human beings having a spiritual experience. We are spiritual beings having a human experience."

I'm not sure if Jack expected me to clap my hands after that or what but I tried to make the face of someone who has just heard some pretty deep shit. Or at least what I think that kind of a face would look like.

"Wow." It's all I could come up with. A random "wow" was the best I had. Okay, so the guy isn't perfect. But who is, right?

"…to learn how to draw upon the higher knowledge already within."

Jesus, I must have tuned out for a minute as I've now lost the thread. I smile and nod and hope to Christ he's going to change the subject soon. But Jack's talk about the Rosicrucians' belief system isn't the only stuff he says that sounds wrong to me. One time he said that my sisters' commitment to complete and utter unquestioning loyalty to each other is unhealthy.

"You're wrong," I said without even thinking. "Our loyalty to each other is what helps make us strong." I didn't tell him that there's no accumulated debt when you borrow from a sister, either. Loyalty. Blind loyalty. That's all we ask of each other.

"The problem with your family," says Jack, as if I asked him what the "problem" is with my family, "is that making loyalty the most important goal in life means one member can't elevate above the rest. You all sink or rise together, which means everyone sinks to the lowest level instead of rising to the highest."

Like I already said, he isn't perfect. He's a psych major at McGill. I try not to hold it too much against him.

They've recently opened a restaurant downtown called McDonald's. They sell cheeseburgers there really cheap. I went there not long after they opened with my sister Julia and we sat at one of the booths for a good ten minutes before we noticed that no one was coming to the tables to serve anyone. People would walk in and go right up to the cash and order. Then stand and wait until the food was all cooked and wrapped up like a present in Styrofoam and placed on a red plastic tray. This place is pretty smart. They make you do half the work for your food. When Julia and I went up and tried to order a hot dog they looked at us like they weren't sure if we were joking or not.

"What? No more hot dogs left?" I said it all nicely and polite. I felt sorry for the girl who was at the cash as they had forced her to wear a plastic looking orange outfit with a paper hat. Her life was already horrible enough. She smiled and said she was sorry but they don't sell hot dogs but would I like to consider one of their other sandwiches? And would I like a pie with that? It felt weird, I admit, to pay good money just for a sandwich but okay, I'm in a lineup now and feeling a little self-conscious so I ask the smiling girl in her plastic suit what kind of sandwiches do they sell.

"We have Big Macs and Filet-O-Fish and…" the girl is listing all kinds of strange sounding stuff and none of the names give away much information on what might be slapped between the bread, expect for the fish fillet but who the hell wants to eat a sandwich with fish stuck in the middle of it? It feels like it's too late now to back away and not order anything so I ask her if I can get a fry, please, and no sandwich, thank you very much. Then my sister Julia looks at her like a cat in an alleyway caught in the beam of a flashlight on firecracker night in the Point, and

I decide to save her and say she'll have the same, thanks. But then the girl makes it all complicated again when she asks, "What would you like to drink with that?"

Of course, I have to be an asshole and without thinking say, "Oh, a Molson X would hit the spot, thanks!" Only Julia gives a nervous laugh and now the jerk behind me in the line is muttering about me.

"What's your problem, asshole?" I say to the girl behind me, and she stares right through me, like she's deaf and dumb and I'm invisible.

Julia quickly orders two cokes, please, and everyone seems relieved that we're done ordering. Until the robot at the cash in her plastic suit can't seem to help herself and asks us again, "Did you want some pie with that?"

Later, as we sat at our futuristic looking table with its bright orange chairs that are actually attached somehow to the table, I have to admit that the French fries are perfect. They're skinny and salty and not greasy at all. Up until that moment, I thought I only liked the fat French fries. These ones are good. The coke tastes a bit funny and seems like it's half water and ice, but it's super cold and more than any one person could drink, anyway. As Julia and I almost finish I notice that the other customers are actually cleaning their tables before they leave. Holy fuck. What a racket. Line up like you're punching in for work, order food with names you're forced to use or else apparently no one knows what the fuck you're talking about, then not only do you have to carry it to your own table, you gotta clean up and throw out your garbage. Way to fuck up something that should be easy. It's obvious this place won't last. People just won't put up with this kind of bullshit for long. I do like the fries, though, but I especially like the foam containers everything is served in. I keep mine and ask Julia if I can have hers unless she's planning on keeping hers as well. It's nicer than any containers I have at my place and I know I can use it again. After eating her fries, Julia went back up to the cash when there wasn't anyone else to line up behind and ordered one of their hamburgers. She offered me a bite and I thought it tasted like nothing but bun and lettuce. But she loved it and was nice about giving me the cute container it came in once she was finished. So instead of me worrying about what in hell to make for him and how to cook it, why can't Jack and I just go to McDonald's and then have the whole food thing be over with?

"Do you ever miss the Point?" asks Julia.

Miss the Point? What's there to miss?

"Uh, I miss some of the people," I say. "What about you?"

Julia also lives with her boyfriend, Matt, far away from the Point. She'd probably say I'm wrong but I know she hates having to bring him there for any reason, even to see Uncle Patrick. I know she's embarrassed and worried about what Matt might think if he sees too much down there. I want to tell her that she's wrong, that Matt is really cool about the Point, that he wouldn't judge her at all.

"You know he told Jack that our dad is like Archie Bunker, right?" says Julia.

Archie fucking Bunker? That old balding racist guy on TV? The one who calls his son-in-law a "meathead, dead from the neck up"? Why does she want me to hate Matt?

"Jack thinks Dad is amazing," I tell Julia.

Matt likes to drop his smart shit like a stun grenade, then leave the room before anyone can react.

"Is Matt gay?" I ask, just to be an asshole.

"What? Gay? No. Matt is not gay," says Julia. "I'll see you later," and she gets up to leave.

I wish I could take back the question about Matt. I know he's not gay. We're at her bus stop now and I can see the bus is less than half a block away. I give her arm a small squeeze and than watch through the windows as Julia gets on the bus and finds herself a seat. I wait but she doesn't look out at the window for my wave goodbye.

Who the hell is Matt, anyway? So what if he's so good-looking I feel a little nervous even talking to him. I should tell Julia what Dad thinks about her dating a Pepper. Even if he does go to McGill, fuck him. Now I wish I had thought to ask her what she had said when Matt said that. I don't think Julia looks at loyalty in the same way that I do. Or maybe it's just part of her way of pretending she grew up somewhere else.

"I can't fake agreeing with something when I don't agree at all," says Julia.

85

Maybe that's why Julia is also one of the smart ones in my family? She's doing well in nursing school. Like Ruth, one day she announced she wanted to be a nurse, just like Annie.

"I'm not copying anyone!" said Julia when I asked why she was copying Annie and Ruth.

"I've always wanted to be a nurse. Just because I didn't tell you doesn't mean I haven't been thinking about it all along. Even way before Annie ever did."

The smirk on her face makes me want to smack her.

"What do you want to be when you grow up?"

Only Julia can ask a simple question in such a way that makes you feel like she's somehow managed to give you a major insult along the way. I know there's no good answer. No matter what I say, her smirk will make it clear it's obviously a really dumb thing to want to be.

I stare at the direction her bus drove off in for a long time.

When I finally get home I realize I still need to figure out a ton of important details about my date with Jack. I have decisions to make. Like, what should I wear for the dinner I'm going to try and make for Jack?

"You could just wear that yellow top with the strings in the front and then he won't care what you cook or serve him," says Annie with a grin, later, and I realize she's right. Jack doesn't really care about the food or what he eats when he's with me. We've got better stuff to do.

When he shows up for dinner, I'm suddenly no longer feeling all nervous about what he's going to think of the food. I want him to think I'm as perfect as he is, even though I'm not even close, of course.

"Come here," says Jack, after looking at he table and then turning back to me. But I'm already there.

My first week at Dawson College has been one of the scariest things I've done. I couldn't believe it when I first got a letter saying I had won the fucking lottery and they were going to let my dumb ass in there. Okay, it didn't say it that way exactly, but you get the point. The huge envelope included a mountain of papers on how to register for classes and programs and I started to realize I was about to become a college dropout before I had even started.

"I can help you!" said Annie, after looking through the pile of papers. "Come on, we'll do it together!"

86

I should have known to ask Annie for help right from the start. This is exactly her kind of thing. First, figure out which classes I'm allowed to take, then make sure they fit on a time schedule that will mean not registering for two classes at the same time by mistake, then figure out where they are on the damn campus and which textbooks I'd need to order and then go and pick up. Whew. To Annie, somehow this is all like math, and math is something Annie knows better than any other person on the planet. It's her second language. Or, actually, maybe her first.

"So which classes do you want to take?" asks Annie.

She truly loves this shit. It felt wrong that she wouldn't be going to college right along with me. Or even instead of me. Everyone knows she's the smartest and hardest working one in the family. It's like she read it on my face.

"Don't be silly," she says. "You know I'm leaving for Halifax soon."

She said "Halifax" all casual, like it was normal for her to be moving so far away and joining the goddamn army. Annie? Of all the people on the planet, my Annie was going to be… a solider?

"No," says Annie, reading my thoughts again. "I'm going to be a nurse. You know that."

"Tell me again why you can't do nursing school here like Ruth and Julia, why you have to go so far way to do it?"

I want to tell Annie she could move to LaSalle. That she doesn't have to go to the moon just to get away from the Point. She can live with me. Damn it. What in hell am I going to do without her in my life?

"Jack will help you. So will Ruth," says Annie.

I'd started to go through the brochures, and then spent the next couple of hours reading course descriptions out loud so Annie and I could laugh.

"Oh, here's one I really need!" I said, then read it out loud to Annie, "Yeah, it's called, I swear to God, 'Cultural and Political Geography,' I shit you not."

"Political? How is geography political?"

"I guess 'cause it's in college? Wait. Let me read you exactly what it says here. 'This course introduces students to basic geographical concepts and examines current problems of our time, for example, resource-based competition, from a spatial perspective…' " Annie is trying to interrupt but I hold up a hand for her to wait. " '…Students are required to complete a research paper demonstrating their understanding of the interplay of cultural, economic and political changes taking place in a specific region.' "

"What the hell?" says Annie. "Do you go to college so that by the time you're done, you know what the hell that all meant? Or do you have to already know what that means?"

"Damn, Annie, if I already knew what that fucking shit meant I wouldn't need any college!"

I was just glad to see that college classes on geography don't make you sit there while a professor stands at the front of the class and uses a yardstick to point to different shapes on the world map and make you call out "Brazil!" Or "Hawaii!"

I've been accepted into the program they call "Social Service," which is kind of like social work for dummies. You know, the students who aren't good or connected or rich enough to go into real social work, at McGill University. But the program at Dawson is one year shorter, a hell of a lot cheaper, and they helped me to get a part-time job to help pay for everything after I told them during my interview that my mom had told me I had to move out if I was going to put on airs and go to college. I've already been doing the job for a couple of weeks now and can't believe how much they pay me to work with kids who have all kinds of problems. Not like the problems kids had at the camp I worked for each summer, Camp Amy Molson. Most of those problems at the camp came from being abused and poor and in and out of foster care. I went there myself every summer for years when I was a kid and then got to work there starting when I was 15. These kids at my new job, though? They aren't able to talk, most can't walk, and none of them can take a shit or care for themselves alone in the bathroom. The staff told me these kids were born this way. None of it was from being poor or being abused by uncles or neighbourhood pervs, or moms who used drugs or drank too much while they were pregnant. These were kids that God just wasn't paying attention to, I guess, so their arms didn't know to grow and their legs were just flappy and soft. Even though these kids' moms sang them songs as babies, held and loved them like every other mom, they just didn't grow right. So now they're all living together in a large group home near the metro station in Verdun and I get to work with them four nights a week and one day on the weekend, making more money than I've ever seen in my life. It's like, crazy.

"You don't need college now," said Ruth after she heard about my first paycheque.

To be honest, I didn't know what to say. I mean, really, why was I going to college, anyway? Sure, I wanted to get smarter but it was also, if not mainly, to get a good job, right? But then again, this job isn't the kind of thing I can see myself doing for a really long time. It's just way too depressing. I mean, when one of the kids finally learned how to drop his dirty fork into the sink after supper, after weeks and weeks of training, with the staff handing him a Smartie for each and every step he slowly took closer and closer to the sink with me holding my breath the entire time as he looked like he was going to fall off his high-tech crutches at any second, everyone cheered like he was close to reaching the finish line at the Olympics. When his fork finally made that loud clinking sound as it hit the bottom of the sink, he didn't even flinch. As far as I could tell, he didn't give two shits about reaching this fork-in-the-sink goal and might not have even known he had. I think he would've washed the windows, moved furniture around, or shit in the toilet instead of his huge diaper if it had meant getting more of those Smarties. And really, it's not like he's gonna need to learn how to drop dirty forks for his own apartment one day. Once these kids arrive here it's pretty much a life sentence. All of them stay put until they either die—and some do—or eventually get transferred to an "adult facility" once they've passed a certain age. So the whole fork in the sink thing seemed kind of dumb to me. What would his mom, the one who used to sing to him when he was a baby, think if she knew that after weeks and weeks of practice, and ten million Smarties later, her baby could now toss his fork into a sink, surrounded by a bunch of equally clueless, diaper-wearing teens? And not even know he had done it? I wonder what that kid would have wanted to learn how to do, if somebody could find a way to ask him? I'm not sure, but I bet it wouldn't be how to toss a fork into the sink.

One day I notice one of the female patients, Carol, has a bandage on her lower stomach. She keeps picking at it and the staff keep trying to distract her from pulling at it.

"What happened? What's up with Carol?" I ask one of the nurses.

Turns out she'd been sterilized. Apparently all the females are once they reach a certain age. I'm not sure if it's so they'll be easier to help keep clean without their monthly flow, or, as one of my sisters wondered, to stop them from getting pregnant. But then, how can they get pregnant, right? Who would be having sex with any of them? I'm starting to hate working there. One time I had just arrived for my shift and found out my unit was at the pool. I was a few minutes late so I didn't even take off my winter coat or boots. Just rushed down to the pool. The kids love the pool but it means everyone is needed on deck. These kids can't walk but they can float around in the water, thanks to life jackets, and most of them love it. The unit head is annoyed with me when I show up.

"You're late," she says.

She's in a bathing suit and already in the water, holding up one of the kids.

"Watch him for a minute," she says and pulls herself out of the water. "The rest of them are in the showers."

As she walks away I look at Billy, the kid still floating in the water, and wonder where to stick my coat and boots. I look away at the bench against the wall for a second and debate if I can just toss my stuff over. Then I look back at Billy and he's not floating on top of the water anymore. He's somehow pulled his life jacket off and is now fully underwater, facing up. As I rush to the edge of the pool I can see his face. He's staring right up at me as I jump into the pool. It's not deep, just barely above my waist, and the water is warm. As I yank him up, clearing his face of the water, I hear someone yelling.

"What the hell are you doing?"

The unit head is back.

"He was under the water," I say, trying to push him onto the ledge on the inside of the pool. She drops back into the water next to him, yanks him from me, and pulls his life jacket back on with one hand.

90

"He does this all the time," she hisses at me. "He just likes to stare up at the ceiling from a few inches under. He was fine!"

It's hard to get out of the water. My winter coat is waterlogged and weighs a ton. My boots are filled with water and my brown cords are turning a faint green right before my eyes.

"Oh, for Christ's sake!"

The unit head is looking at me with disgust. "Look what you've done to yourself."

I feel so embarrassed, I'm speechless. I just want to run away. It's like I shit myself and she can tell.

"You better go to the nursing station and see if they have something you can put on," she says, and then turns back to Billy. "Come on, buddy, time to get out of the pool. Lunch!"

For days, I can feel the looks and see the smirks on everyone's face whenever they see me. Yeah, I'm that idiot. The one who jumped in the pool to "save" a kid who didn't need any saving at all. I desperately wish I could quit. They offer non-stop advice now, too.

"Hey, if one of the kids look like they're in trouble, or you think you smell smoke, don't be 'saving' their life or pulling any fire alarms until you run it past one of us first, okay?"

It never gets old. I've learned to ignore the laughter. I just nod my head, acknowledging that I get it. I'm a fucking fool. I want to quit. Every single shift I think about it. I think about calling in sick, at least. For the rest of my life. I hate the patients. I hate the staff. I hate the smells. Pee and baby powder. I feel like one of the patients now. I can't do anything right and need someone to practically wipe my ass now. The only problem is, I can't quit and I know it. At least, not yet. It's not only paying my share of the rent, it's also paying for all my school books, groceries, and monthly bus pass, too. So yeah, I've learned to become part of the cheering section for Wonder Fork Boy. And remind myself to pretend not to notice anymore if I ever think someone might be drowning or on fire. Or anything else at all.

"What other classes do you think you're going to register for?" asked Annie. "We need to get all of the choices written down on here," she said, holding up my registration form.

The three-year program at Dawson I got into is advertised as "Human

Rights. Social Justice. Changing Lives. If these words speak to you, then Dawson's Social Service Program is where you belong."

Hell, who wouldn't want to change lives, right?

"What about this course," I say to Annie. "The one called 'Human Development'?"

"Read the course description out loud," says Annie. "What does it say?"

None of it really makes any sense to me, honestly.

"This course provides an introduction to human development through an exploration of lifelong changes that occur from conception to death."

Okay, "from conception to death," which I think means we'd be looking at what happens from the moment people fuck, a baby is born, and then it grows up and eventually dies. Pretty cool, right? But that wasn't everything.

"Each stage of the life-cycle will be examined through the cognitive, psychosocial and emotional influences on human development…"

It said more but I was starting to sound like I was being fake and phoney, reading all that shit out loud to Annie. But yeah, I was excited about getting started, knowing I'd one day really know what the hell all those words actually meant. I couldn't wait to see me on the other side.

"Let's see which classes you're allowed to smoke in," said Annie.

At Dawson, it's listed in the course descriptions which professors are fussy about you smoking in class and which ones don't give a shit. All things being equal, I was going to choose the classes where I could sit and smoke at my desk, of course. Hell, forget all things being equal. First, which one allowed us to smoke? Second, which one was in my program? Third, Mickey Mouse sounding, please.

Jack told me I should take a couple of the courses that he did before. He's at McGill now, but was at Dawson last year. He did the coursework you need to apply to university so he didn't do any of the programs, just a general arts certificate. I know I'd never be able to handle university, anyway, so Dawson's fake social worker program is just my speed. And they don't even let you smoke at McGill, the stuck-up fuckers.

"Are you smoking?" asked Jack when I got home from school. I never do it in our apartment. Jack hates smoking and won't even share a joint with me. I always brush my teeth in the bathroom at school or work before I come home so I have a second to decide what to say. Does he already know? Or is he fishing? If I say yes, it will mean a boring lecture. If I say no and he already knows I did, it'll be a stressful lecture about not lying, the importance of honesty in a relationship, blah, blah. I decide to go with a question instead.

"Why are you asking?"

"Stop being evasive and just answer the question."

Jack looks majorly pissed off. Damn it. Here comes the boring lecture. If it's not my smoking it's my swearing, though I really do try to never swear around Jack at all. I know he thinks it makes me sound lowbrow or something.

"Word choices matter," he'll say, which means I must have dropped the f-bomb in a sentence without even realizing it, though I'm working real hard on not doing that anymore.

"It deeply impacts how others view you," says Jack. I know not to say, "Who gives a shit?" But the no-smoking thing is getting tiresome. He's got the nose of a hound. I try to argue my case.

"Yeah, but not much and not often! And I'm going to quit, right now, seriously. I gave the rest of my pack to my sister Annie. Seriously!"

Why do I think if I say it fast it will sound more true? I take a big breath.

"You know, if we ever break up, this will be the reason. You know that, right?" says Jack.

Shit. Well, fuck me. So much for the boring lecture. Nothing like going straight for the pin and pulling that sucker right out. Now I'm pissed.

"You know I don't respond well to threats, right? If me having an occasional puff of a cigarette is enough to make you dump me, well then, I guess we're done."

And I mean it, too. I mean, I love Jack. I really do. I feel like I've won some kind of lottery every single time I wake up and see him sleeping next to me. There is no question he is the best thing that has ever happened to me. But threaten me? Stop loving me because of something like smoking? Say you'll leave me? Fuck you, 'cause I'm already gone.

"Wait a minute," says Jack. "Don't get that look on your face, you know…"

"I know we won't make it, I agree," I say.

And I'm not playing.

"No, we won't make it if you choose for us not to make it!" says Jack. "And your choice to keep on smoking, despite what I've said about how I feel about that, tells me YOU have made a choice to abandon this relationship, not ME. So don't try and turn this around and put it on me. This? This is on you!"

He doesn't get that I won't argue about this. I'm already done.

"Yup, you're right. It's on me," I shrug.

Just 'cause I'm done doesn't mean I won't try and bug the shit out of him as much as I can. Fucker.

"Oh, for god's sake, stop that! Don't do that!"

"Do what?" I feel completely calm now. Not mad. Not scared. Not really.

"That thing you do when you start to feel threatened at all. Playing dead…"

"I'm not feeling 'threatened,' or playing…"

"Forget it," snaps Jack. "Let's talk about this later."

I know my amused tone is starting to push his buttons and now he's afraid of saying something he'll regret. He doesn't seem to get that he can't make it any worse. It's already as bad as it can get. I'm done.

"Sure, no problem." I leave the apartment again. I wanna have a smoke.

Chapter Six

BECAUSE I'VE WORKED AT Camp Amy Molson for a bunch of summers in a row now, the director has asked me if I'd be willing to come to one of the board meetings and talk about my experiences with the camp, both as a camper and a member of the staff.

"It will be very causal," she says. "Just a nice dinner and some drinks and maybe you could give a short talk and just answer a few of their questions."

I should have known better, of course, but I admit I'm curious. The board of directors are the rich people behind the scenes who do most of the camp's fundraising and help keep it running year after year.

"Sure, I'd be happy to!" I say. And two weeks later, I'm sitting in the living room of a board member while she's serving all of us, including me, tea from a silver teapot into the fanciest looking teeny cups and small plates I've ever seen in my life. After I first sat down on her sofa I sank so low I wanted to say thanks for the warning about the quicksand couch. When she hands me a cup I take it without thinking, even though I consider tea to be one of those shitty drinks you pretend to like so you don't offend the people who swear by it. Nanny always serves tea that's been gently boiling on her stove for the entire day so I'm used to it being hot. This tea is just warm and I'm nervous about the cup. I keep reminding myself not to accidentally bite the rim and end up with a sliver of that gold porcelain in my mouth. The handle seems fragile as hell and I'm afraid to stick my finger in it so I hold it carefully between my thumb and finger. I'm secretly pleased when I realize my pinky is sticking out like the Queen's. Just as I take a small sip, though, I see what looks like a small handful of old lady pubes sitting on top of the tea. A bunch of fine grey hairs all balled up, floating on top of my fucking tea. What the fuck?

I suddenly realize that they're not old lady pubes—it's dust. The rich old lady serving the tea doesn't use these fancy-pancy cups all that often. Maybe that means she's trying to impress me, at least?

It'll look rude to not drink the tea, so I decide to just get it over with as quickly as possible and gulp all the old lady pubes down. When the old biddy asks me if I want more I wonder for a second if she's messing with me, then catch myself and know to say no thanks and just smile. A few minutes later, she stands up and asks everyone to please follow her to the dining room as dinner is now ready to be served, and everyone moves so quickly I wonder if they worry there might not be enough chairs to go around. I'm relieved to see there's not only plenty of chairs but there's also enough forks and knives and plates in front of each chair to serve three people. I have a pile of plates in front of me, like a set of those Russian dolls. A big gold one on the bottom topped by a white and then another small silver one to the side. I also have an army of glasses and cups. After some guy pours me water, another brings me the beer I ask for and sets it next to the wineglass in front of my tiny plate.

The food is pure shit, of course. After they serve us some stuff they call a salad, which is weird since there isn't even any lettuce in it at all, just cucumber slices and some green round thing with black dots that looked like mouse shit, then they bring out a plate for each of us with two of the tiniest chickens I've ever seen in my life, side by side, surrounded by teeny potatoes. For each of us! We each got our own personal fucking teeny chickens. I feel like I should name mine, or something. I swear, they must have a rich person's store they all go to that sells only food miniatures or something. I wonder where these tiny chickens even come from. Their eggs must look like white peas.

The other guests don't even eat the best part. They all just pull back the crispy skin and eat the stuff underneath. When I was gnawing away on what is the tiniest chicken wing I've ever seen, never mind tried to eat, some of them looked at me like *I* was the weirdo.

I also made the mistake of faking admiration for the grandfather clock I saw in the entrance of the home when I first arrived. Big mistake.

"Holy fuck, everything that is holy. Rich people sure do love their fucking grandfather clocks, right?"

And it's true. I've seen three of them now in rich people's homes, all volunteers and board members in Westmount, of course, and they always have some long and boring story attached to them. Gives them something to talk about, I guess? Its almost creepy, though, how their stories sound like the clock survived some traumatic ordeal before finally being "rescued" and ending up in their loving home forever. Like a ratty dog from a shelter like the SPCA, or a foster kid.

"This big fellow here? This is a nineteenth-century Rustic Black Forest Grandfather Clock comprised of walnut which, as you can see, is elaborately carved with oak leaves and beams in high relief."

I knew not to volunteer that I now hated the clock even more. And, by the way, isn't Black Forest a kind of cake? Since when is it a damn clock, right? I guess my blank look somehow screamed "tell me more boring shit about your fucking clock" to the rich guy.

"They say that grandfather clocks are as old as time but, strictly speaking, this isn't quite accurate, of course."

Of course.

"These clocks were first built in the 1600s. However, as we know, time itself is a concept which predates this by many, many years."

Thank god the camp director is a normal, regular person. She's the only one there who has asked me a single question so far. I'm feeling a little sorry for her. She's really trying so hard.

"Kathy? Maybe you could tell us about your own... history with the camp?"

So over tiny cakes and more of that tea with the old lady pubes, I sell my soul to the Devil and tell them all about how going to the camp, first as a kid at four, while my mom worked in the kitchen, meant plenty of good food and lots of fun in the lake and on the sports field. And then how, later, much later, I worked as a counsellor in training and so on, for many more summers, including being a cabin counsellor and, eventually, an activity leader. I leave out the part about me being the Nature Lore instructor on program staff one summer. They don't need to know about that moment I had a fucking grass snake hanging off my finger while the campers were all laughing as I shrieked, "LET GO OF MY FINGER, YOU FUCKER!"

After the millions of plates and glasses and pieces of cutlery have been cleared from the table, the director makes a big and embarrassing production of introducing me again, reminding them, like maybe half of them are senile or something, that I'd been a camper for years, way before I'd ever even worked at the camp. Then she looks at me and nods for me to begin. Shit. I thought I'd already said enough stuff to make them feel good about themselves.

I start by first telling them how if I had known going in what to *really* expect as a staff member, I might not have made it past the first few days. I mean, honestly, who would willingly sign up to come to a place that means working 24/7 for two weeks at a stretch, while often sleep-deprived, with no electricity, about ten seconds a day to brush your teeth and go to the bathroom, while sharing a cabin with a bunch of kids, who, the first few days of camp, will test you for everything you're worth? They all laugh like I've made a joke.

I shrug it off and continue.

"I remember during pre-camp staff training the camp director talked about how some of these kids would need our help in 'getting out of their own way,'" I say.

I don't focus on any particular face at the table. I'm afraid if I read something in the Staff Training Manual or see the wrong thing I might say something stupid that I won't be able to take back. These are the people who make the camp possible. I don't have to like them. But I do have to respect that they have a lot of power.

"We were warned that many of these kids could be bringing some emotional baggage with them to camp," I continue, "and the camp director stressed the importance of us staff helping these kids to be able to be, well, *kids* during their time at Camp Amy Molson."

I realize a few people are smiling and nodding at me. I take a huge breath and decide to go for it.

"It was at Camp Amy Molson, while a camper, that I learned to have faith in this world as I realized that not everyone wants to hurt kids and, in fact, some just want to love them and help them have fun. As a child, I spent every fall and winter waiting for summer so I could go back to the place I felt happiest and safest in the world."

I'm done. I feel weird and out of breath now. One of the board members at the far end of the table holds up his wineglass.

"And this is why we also care so much about the camp."

Okay, I admit it. Maybe not every rich person is an asshole. It feels weird but I actually really like going to all of my classes at Dawson. I'm secretly embarrassed by how much I love it. I like my bag and my pens and highlighters and papers and I even like the textbooks I have to read. I like flipping open my notebook when it's time to take notes. I love my tiny ashtray and being able to smoke and drink coffee while soaking up stuff. I feel like I'm in a slow, but still kind of interesting, cool movie. The teachers are all really good at explaining things and making stuff sound interesting. The sociology professor talks about how important other people are in helping to make us who we are. Good and bad.

"Our entire existence is defined by our relationships with others and until we understand those relationships, we can't even begin to understand ourselves or the world around us."

Pretty cool, right?

The same prof talks about gender all the time as well, saying people often make the mistake of thinking the words "sex" and "gender" are the same thing. If I was the type to put my hand up in class, and I'm not, I would have said I've never thought they mean the same thing. 'Cause until that class, I'm really sure I never used the word gender before in any way. But this prof talks about how sex is something we *do*, and gender is something we *are*. Well, assuming I understood what he was saying, and I never assume I do. I'm probably the only one in the class who kept moving around in my chair not sure where to look when he said things like "ejaculation" and "the deepest recesses of the vagina."

"Fuck off!" says Annie. "A teacher said that? Out loud? In front of everybody? Screw the army. I gotta go to Dawson."

And honestly? She'd love it. All of my sisters would. I'm learning about shit I didn't even know I wanted to learn.

"The term 'meritocracy' describes a society in which resources are distributed fairly on the basis of merit. Which fails to take into account how one's social location in terms of race and gender and class affect one's potential for achievement."

Okay, so I had to write that one down and read it about a million times and think about it for a while before it could slowly dawn on me what it meant.

If someone had told me a few years ago that one day my mom would be off welfare, working full-time at the clinic in the Point and back living with my dad, I would have said no fucking way. I mean, okay, maybe back with Dad. Maybe. They've been doing that back and forth dance with each other forever now. As soon as Mom would finally get super fed up and put her foot down and push him away, it would only pull him back tighter. Always. But then something would happen again and Dad would disappear for a while and Mom would just seem to let it go. But now they've been back together for a while. After the clinic hired Mom to be a community health-care worker, whatever the hell that means, she started getting paid enough to tell the welfare office to go fuck itself sideways. She said the best part was knowing she'd never have to let some asshole into our place again to walk around looking for proof of a man being tucked away somewhere, while making nasty little comments about the messy floors and piles of crap lying around everywhere.

After the clinic signed a contract with all of its community workers from the neighbourhood, Mom said she felt more safe than she ever had in her life. I'm not sure why that made her feel safe. Dad could still stroll into the flat whenever he wanted to, and often did. One time he snuck in with a baseball bat in the middle of the night after he had heard a rumour that Mom was sleeping with someone else now. Of course, it didn't matter that they had been broken up for a few years. Just because Dad wasn't sleeping over anymore didn't mean anyone else was allowed to. As Dad crept into the bedroom, the light from the street lamp outside the bedroom window made it just bright enough for him to see that the person lying next to Mom was wearing a bright white bra, so he lowered the baseball bat. He said later he was surprised his laughter didn't wake them both up before he slinked back out. Mom's friend, Mrs. O'Leary, who'd been sleeping over after she told Mom how mad her husband was at her, still doesn't know how close she came to never being able to walk straight again.

Mom is pretty much set now, even though she still gives away half her paycheque each and every payday.

"I'm making a ridiculous salary, of course I have to share it!" says Mom after Dad tells her to stop being stupid. "How can I keep all that money when so many other people don't have anything?" she says.

It's not long before Dad isn't the only one waiting for Mom outside the clinic on payday.

"I'll meet you on Wellington Street, okay?" says Mom to the small group that's collected outside. Then she goes into the Royal Bank and gets a bunch of fives and tens and when she comes back out on Wellington Street, hands them out like they're candy on Halloween.

"You're an idiot," says Dad. "You're just encouraging them."

I wish Mom were willing to give some of that candy to us girls, though.

"One of my classes says that kindergarten is like 'academic boot camp' for kids," I say to Annie. I know she'll find this as interesting an idea as I do. I can tell I have her full attention.

"Seriously," I continued, "some guy called Harry Gracey says the real purpose of kindergarten is to teach kids from the time they're little how to be perfect students and follow the rules, know how to behave in a school setting and shit."

"So I guess that's why kids like us from the Point don't always do so well in school?" laughs Annie. "We didn't learn any of those rules about how to behave and be 'perfect' students."

I tell Annie how students even learn to respect bells and alarms going off in school.

"That's in the rich kids' school, though, right?"

I know exactly what Annie means. We didn't learn about any of that shit at Lorne School in the Point. Or at least I didn't. Maybe I was skipping that day, the day they taught us that when a bell goes off you're supposed to, well, do something. Something other than give it the finger and just keep on doing whatever you were doing. I must have also missed the day they taught us that no matter how mean or dumb-ass a teacher is, you have to give them a pass *just* 'cause they're a teacher.

Can you understand why I'm loving Dawson College? Damn, I wish everyone I know from the Point could join me in some of these classes. They'd also learn, like I am, that the Point isn't the bad guy in this bullshit. I've been thinking for years how bad I want to escape the Point and now that I have, I realize it was never really the Point.

"We construct ghettos and gangs and the poor as enemies and threats, but they're a symptom of the disease of neo-liberalism," my sociology prof says one day. I have to write it down word for word so that I can study it later and try to figure out what the hell it means. Or at least be able to parrot those sentences in my papers so it will maybe look like I know what's going on.

"What else?" asks Annie. "Go ahead. Seriously. For real. Freak me out."

I tell Annie how at Dawson they actually want you to call out the profs when you think they're full of shit.

"Not in a rude way, of course, and you can't actually say it's pure bullshit. But they seriously like you more if you put up your hand and question them. You know, let them know you aren't convinced. At least not yet."

"Wow. So you get to tell them when you actually disagree? That's amazing!"

I feel embarrassed that Annie thinks I meant I'm always arguing stuff with the profs. I don't want her to know this but I'm super quiet in class. I just sit there and listen to everything. I smoke and tap my ashes into the small red travelling ashtray that Annie gave me as a graduation gift after I finished high school, but I never actually say anything. I don't even know how to talk like these people. They already know how they feel about everything. None of them ever seem surprised or impressed by anything, either. Half the time I have to remind myself not to yell out, "Holy fuck, for real?" and to close my gaping mouth when something really catches me off guard. How come no one has ever told me any of this stuff? It makes me wonder what I used to think or talk about before I'd heard about any of this shit. When the prof said something about "the male gaze" one day I wanted to make jokes about that being my favourite kind of donut, minus the sprinkles on top, ha ha, But thank god I knew to keep my stupid mouth shut. One of my classes even explained why they don't eat any of the cows wandering all around in India, even though people are starving to death. Okay, to be fair, I never wondered about that before. I don't think I even knew they were starving to death in some parts of India before taking this class, and for sure didn't know they had cows wandering freely around, either. But still, this is what I mean. I'm learning about all kinds of stuff I didn't know I didn't know and didn't know to want to know. Know what I mean?

"What do you mean the cows are 'sacred' there?"

Annie is fascinated as I try and give her a short version of what I'd been learning about this in a class called World Views, East and West. I'd registered for it because it was the only thing left that could fit on my schedule for Friday mornings so I can keep my nights free for work, but in the end, I'm so glad I took the class. It's fucking amazing. The prof has a huge accent and at first I was nervous all the time, worried I'd never know what the fuck he was talking about. I kept thinking the other students must be faking that they could actually understand him and kept trying to catch someone's eye so I could share a look of, what the fuck, right? But within a few classes I suddenly realized I could understand him perfectly and thanked god I never said anything stupid about him to any of the other students. This prof is deeply serious about his shit and has somehow made me give a shit as well. I start to dream of maybe one day being able to travel, maybe even seeing one of those sacred cows myself in person. Wouldn't that be fucking incredible? Me, Kathy Dobson, being able to one day go somewhere outside of Montreal? I never thought I'd ever make it out of the Point. Imagine if I got to go somewhere outside of Canada? Unreal, right? But I don't know. Dawson has a way of making me think maybe anything can happen now. Anything. Maybe.

I'm surprised by how much harder one class is compared to what I had expected. When I first read the Psychology of Sexual Behaviour class description in the Course Selection booklet, I instantly figured it would be easy, Mickey Mouse bullshit. And who wouldn't, right? I figured since I was having sex I'd ace that course. Big mistake. I should have realized Annie was on to something when, after I read the course description to her out loud, she said, "What the fuck does that actually even mean?"

So I read it again, but this time more slowly.

"This course deals with human sexual development and response patterns, addressing both the psychological, physiological and socio-cultural factors shaping and influencing human sexual behaviour. Topics may include anatomy and physiology of the sexual response system, development of gender identity, sexual response patterns and sexual dysfunctions."

I thought the part about the "anatomy of the sexual response" was a kind of "how to" part of the course and since I already know how to, that's why I thought I'd find the class easy.

"What's it mean, though," asked Annie, "where it says 'socio-cultural factors'?"

"I'm thinking it's like comparing how often do French people do it versus English people. You know, which culture fucks the most?"

When I finally went to the first class, I was instantly a little nervous because the professor was so good-looking and younger than all of my other teachers.

"Hey everyone, welcome to what I hope will be your favourite sex class ever!"

Everyone laughed a little, just to be polite. Lame, yes, but he was trying to be friendly.

"If you look at the course syllabus which I have placed on the desks for each of you, please note the warning on page one about the explicit content of some of the movies we will be watching over the next several weeks. If watching other people engage in intercourse is a problem, this might not be the class for you."

Uh, wait a minute. Intercourse? As in, having sex? We're going to be watching other people have sex? On purpose?

During the first movie, which was shown during the very next class, I had to remind myself to breathe a few times. I was so worried I'd be mistaken for one of the girls we were watching in the movie; they were breathing all raggedy and sometimes embarrassingly panting and even breathless. The guys in the movie never made a sound but the females made it impossible to know where to look. What if I looked around the room and accidentally made eye contact with another student? Yet staring at the screen seemed wrong, too. I didn't want to look too into it, but I also didn't want to look somewhere else. I'm sure my face was beet red the entire time. And then, to make it even worse, the first snap quiz asked a lot of questions I actually had to guess. I didn't remember anyone ever explaining the actual length of time of an average female orgasm. I mean, Jesus Christ, how do they even know this shit, anyway? Is some weirdo in a white lab coat actually recording the length of time of a group of women having orgasms and then figuring out the average based on the individual times of each member of the group? Well, as it turns out, the following week in class I learned that, yes, that's exactly what they've done. In a lab. With a bunch of male researchers wearing white lab coats. Perverts, right?

When I realized I could stare at that list of multiple-choice quiz questions all day and still not know the right answers to most of them, I quickly picked what I hoped would give me at least a half shot at a pass. I hated having to walk over to the prof's desk to hand in the quiz. I was the first one done so I had a roomful to watch me as I got up to leave. Is it just me or do other people forget how to walk like a fucking normal human being when you know other people are staring at you? I felt like my ass was moving too much and my legs were taking short donkey steps. Shit.

"Too easy for you?" asked the prof as I handed him my paper.

Okay, what in hell do you say to something like that?

"Yup, I'm a genius," Or instead, "Oh, not at all easy. It was super tough! But I figure I'd rush through it all anyway, and hand it in even though I still have a good half hour that I could be working on it, trying to make sure I come up with the right answers!"

And then there's the final choice, the one I actually went with.

"Huh?"

Then I put down the paper and left the room. Yeah, I'm sure he folded down the corner of my paper so he could check for himself later what my name is. So he can know who the moron in his class is.

This prof is kind of cute in an old guy sort of way. Tall, handsome, and so easygoing you just know he's practiced how to look that cool and blasé about everything. Still, he's kind of hot for an old person. He must be at least in his early thirties. Thank god I didn't blurt out, like I almost did, that I really just want to be a writer and don't care all that much about the other stuff at school. I sent a short story to *Reader's Digest* one time and still have the rejection letter they sent me. It's the first time I submitted anything anywhere and Annie was all worried it might make me feel discouraged.

"That magazine is just a rag, anyway," she said. "The kind you only read while on the toilet and you don't want someone to be taking a shit while they're reading your stuff, anyway!"

I've heard Mom talking about this writer, some guy named Fennario, with her social worker friends because he's from the Point. Well, this

Fennario guy had actually shown up to talk about his work at Dawson and one of my profs had really encouraged all of us to attend the talk. At first, I thought it would be cool, you know? Listen to someone who grew up in the Point and has actually written about it and everything. Sounds like it would be amazing, right? When I got there I was surprised to see dozens of students already standing around him, like he was some rock star at a concert and they couldn't believe they could just reach out and actually be able to touch him. Every time he said something, the group would actually clap and cheer. Like he was announcing the winning numbers for next week's lottery.

"So I decided fuck that, the Man can go to hell," says Fennario and the crowd cheers and laughs and nods their heads and waves their arms. Dad has said this guy is just a goddamn communist and I'm starting to feel annoyed by him myself. He's got the "poor but still tough guy" act down pat. I'm surprised he hasn't rolled up his sleeves yet to show off his tats to this room of hardcore fans who are just looking for more to love about him. The cigarette tucked behind his ear and strategically ripped white under-shirt makes me feel aggressive for some reason. When someone asks him what's the difference between the neighbourhoods of Point St. Charles and LaSalle, I'm stunned when he says there isn't much difference at all.

"They're both working-class neighbourhoods," says Fennario. "I'd say they're pretty much the same."

Of course, I can't help myself and raise my hand. When he looks in my direction, I don't wait for him to call on me.

"How can you say those two neighbourhoods are the same?" I ask. "I mean, in the Point, practically everyone is on welfare and in LaSalle you have some people on welfare, sure, but mostly people have jobs."

Take that, David Fennario, and thank you Dawson College for teaching me all those important details just last week, about the Point having the highest rate of welfare recipients in Montreal, all crowded into one square mile.

"And who are you?" he asks, his eyes burning a hole into my forehead. Oh, now he wants background info before he answers a question? For the life of me, I still don't know why I didn't just make up a name on the spot, and instead, I say who I am and then stare back at him, waiting for him to challenge my facts or stats.

"Your last name is Dobson?" he asks.

"Uh, right."

"Is your mom Eileen Dobson?"

Jesus. She follows me everywhere.

"Um, yeah," I admit and suddenly realize that his dozens of fans have fallen silent and everyone is now staring at me.

"She's cool," announces Fennario, like he's the god of deciding who is cool and who is not. "Your mom, Eileen. She works hard to make a difference and change the conditions of the People. I like her. Please tell her I said hello."

And with that, he's done with me and calls on the next student who, as it turns out, just wants to gush about how "authentic" his working-class voice is in his book *Without a Parachute*.

"Are you making a bunch of friends at college?" asks Annie.

I understand why she'd think I am. TV makes college look like half the time you're drinking and the other half you're being pawed at by some of the school's football players at parties. I think that's how it maybe works in the States. At Dawson they don't even have a football team, and as for making new friends?

"Yeah," I tell Annie, "I talked to someone in my class yesterday. They seemed pretty cool."

I had said "sure" to another student when they asked if they could borrow my eraser for a second, then "no problem" a minute later after they said thanks and handed it back. Yup, we're definitely on track to become best friends.

I'm pretty much invisible in class. Even the profs don't seem to see me.

"Tons and tons of friends," I say to Annie.

"They all hate you, right?" says Annie, and she smiles.

Annie is the one that everyone instantly likes and wants to be friends with. She can talk to pretty much anybody. Old people, young people, even French people. Everyone loves Annie. But of course, why wouldn't they? I hate it when I have to meet any of Jack's friends. I never know what to say to any of them. One time we went to a party in someone's basement and a girl kept laughing and touching Jack's arm. She didn't seem to hear me when I said hello after Jack introduced me. It bugged the shit out of me that he had just said I was Kathy, and didn't say I was his girlfriend. I know if I complained about it later, though, I'd get the whole speech about jealousy being such an unattractive trait, blah, blah, blah. When we were leaving I got a bit ahead of Jack to the door and when I looked back I could see her speaking closely into his ear, her hand leaning on his chest. Jack put his head back and laughed and it felt like someone had just punched me right in the gut. I couldn't breathe for a few seconds and felt like I could barf right then and there. When he came towards me she was still hanging off him and when they reached me at the door, the smile left her eyes and she just stared.

"This is Pascale," said Jack. "We're going to give her a lift home. It's on our way."

She ignored me as she got into the back seat and then tapped Jack on the shoulder.

"Hey, why don't you put on CJAD?"

When Jack grinned at her in his mirror and then started looking for the station, I seriously wondered for just a second if I was in a dream. It was like they both had forgotten I was there. Suddenly the sounds of Gloria Gaynor filled the car, singing "I Will Survive."

"Wow, I love that song!" I said without even thinking. It was one of my absolute favourites and had recently hit the Top 10 list. Before Gloria had belted two lines out, though, Jack was twisting the dial to another station. As I turned and looked at him the car was suddenly filled with The Pointer Sisters singing "Fire."

"OHMYGOD!" said Pascale from the back seat, "Don't touch that dial!" and her and Jack both laugh and laugh while I sat quietly in the front seat listening as The Pointer Sisters sing about riding in your car and when we kiss…

"That is such a hot song," laughed Pascale.

She was dancing now. Moving and grooving and making a pouty face with her lips. I wanted to turn around and punch her right in the throat. I waited for Jack to notice that she wasn't wearing her seat belt. He had always given me shit anytime I tried to pretend I had forgotten to put it on. I watched as he checked her out again and again in his mirror.

"You should put on your seat belt," I finally said, twisting around so she couldn't pretend not to hear me. "Seriously," I said. "Put it on."

"Thanks, Mom," she said and then grinned at Jack who was looking at her again in his rear-view mirror. They both laughed as she put her belt on. Maybe Nanny is right. Just because a guy brushes his teeth isn't reason enough to love him.

I don't remember anything else about the drive home. I just tuned them both out. I concentrated instead on not throwing up all over the car. When we got to our place, I was out of the car before Jack could turn off the engine.

"What the hell was that?" asked Jack when he came in a few minutes later.

I ignored him, burying my face in one of my textbooks.

"I'm talking to you! I've never been so embarrassed in my life!"

For Jack, he was almost yelling. It felt good for some reason to hear his angry voice, demanding I answer him. He could have held a knife to my throat and I still wouldn't have made a peep. He was now invisible. The louder he got, the stronger I felt. It was fantastic. I would have had sex with him right then and there had he not been so fixated on being angry with me. It was stupid but I couldn't help myself. I looked up at him and grinned. Then he took the phone into the bathroom. Fuck him, anyway. Sometimes I get paranoid that Jack is cheating on me. I mean I know he isn't, of course. He'd never be that dishonest. The importance of being honest is so big with him I'm sometimes afraid I'm telling a lie even when I know I'm not. But I hate it when he goes into the bathroom with the phone, with the cord under the door, and turns on the water in the sink. I still listen at the door, of course, and try not to breathe so I can hear him over the gushing water. Good thing we don't have to pay for water at our apartment. We'd go broke.

"Who were you talking to?" I ask.

"What?"

"Who were you just talking to on the phone?"

"The phone? Me? Why?"

He's frowning now.

"Just wondering who it was. You were on the phone for a long time."

x

"What? Are you timing my phone calls now?"

"No, no, I just mean that…"

"If we don't have trust in our relationship then we don't have anything at all!" says Jack.

"Yeah, right, sorry. It's just that, well, one of my sisters said…"

"Wait a minute. Are you going to quote one of your sisters to me?"

He says the word "sisters" like I had said I was going to tell him what the neighbour's cat just said to me the other day.

"I don't give a flying heap what any of your sisters think," he says with a sneer, like all of my sisters are so unworthy of any kind of respect, I'm an even bigger dumb ass for daring to mention what one of them actually thinks. Now I'm the one feeling a little out of breath.

"All that matters to me is what you think," says Jack. "And what you think is something you can just relay to me without the middle man of claiming it's what a sister thinks. At least have the intellectual honesty to own what you think. Don't attribute it to someone else."

How does he do that? How does he manage to turn every single argument around so that I'm the moron and he's the damn victim? That I'm somehow attacking him and being incredibly offensive?

"You need to kick the rest of your family out of this relationship," continues Jack. "This is about you. And me. Period."

"My sisters are just trying to…"

"Just stop it. Right there," says Jack. He's holding up both of his hands.

I decide I should probably tell him another time that my period is late. He seems so mad already I don't want to make things worse. Later, when he takes the phone into the bathroom again, I decide to just go out. I need to buy some smokes, anyway.

Chapter Seven

DEALING WITH THE DEAD PERSON is never the hard part about a funeral. It's the living who create all the problems. You've got your criers, the fainters, and then you've got the angry ones; those are the ones that make me the most nervous. They're so mad that their loved one has passed, they're looking for a target to attack—someone to hand all that rage over to. Fortunately, they usually end up sending it all heavenward, calling God a douchebag, piece of shit, thoughtless motherfucker. That was my cousin John after his dad died. John blamed God for the whole thing for months and months. It didn't matter that his dad was shot by the cop he'd been pointing his gun at. Nope. John wasn't even mad at the cop who killed his dad.

"Of course he shot my dad. My dad was gonna shoot him. He had no choice."

But God didn't get a pass on this death. Nope.

"God had a choice," said John. "The fucker. He could've knocked that gun right out of the cop's hand. He could've made the bullets disappear. He could've made them melt right inside the gun and then drip outta the end of the barrel like that glue you can't stop from coming out of the bottle once you've taken that red tip off."

Yup. You need a running start with that conversation. I knew John would be okay at this funeral, though. Instead, it was the funeral director who was being the problem right now.

"Do you have any actual… credentials?" he asks me. His raised eyebrows make me want to kick him in the ass. Before I can answer, he asks another question.

"Where were you ordained? Which church?"

The Church of Canada Post, where all mail-order licenses come from, I want to say but instead, I decide to make it sound worse. "The Church of Love," I reply with a perfectly straight face.

"The Church of… Love?" he asks, needing to hear it again. "What…?"

"As the Apostle Paul wrote," I say, " 'All are able ministers of the new covenant, not of the letter, but of the Spirit; for the letter kills, but the Spirit gives life.' "

I fight the urge to tell the director he should close his mouth.

Whenever someone dies in the Point, the ceremony is nearly always held at this funeral home. The owners are Outsiders, and they don't even try to hide the contempt on their faces.

"I need to get back out there," I say. "They're waiting for me. You don't want them getting restless or to come looking for me." I turned and left his small office.

I hoped he wouldn't follow me back into the chapel. He seemed to be having a hard time keeping the sneer off his face. I knew he was worried about the growing crowd that continued to press into the chapel. They were getting rowdy. A few had started dancing when the Irish Rovers' "Unicorn Song" started blaring out of the ghetto-blaster smuggled in by one of my cousins. Maybe the funeral director was thinking of Sharron Prior's funeral, the teenager from Point St. Charles who years earlier had been brutally raped and murdered. By an Outsider. Say what you want about the Point, what happened to Sharron never would have been done by one of the locals. As the hearse moved slowly down Wellington Street, half the Point rioted, breaking storefront windows, setting buildings on fire and flipping cars. Just about the whole Point was mad at God that day. Some of us still hold it against him. Sharron had been a great girl. Sweet, shy and smart as hell. Her twin baby sisters had sat at the window for two days waiting and watching for their big sister to come home. My mother cried for a long time after we all heard what had happened to Sharron. Not for Sharron, but for Yvonne, Sharron's mother.

"Sharron's already gone," said Mom when I tried to hug her. "But her mom is going to have to live with this agony for the rest of her life."

Yvonne is one of the other moms in the Point working with my mom on trying to make the Point better. Yvonne is a popular and well-known mom in the neighbourhood, and not because of what happened to Sharron. Where my mom is flashy and happy to be the centre of attention, to be interviewed by the media and come up with new ways to stand out, Yvonne is low-key, doesn't seem to need much attention and is happy to stay in the background, as long as stuff happens. And she's someone who works her ass off to help make stuff happen. Sharron was known for helping her mom and being super close to her sisters and little brother. Hell, after selling a ton of tickets she earned the right to a free Leo's Boys and Girls Club jacket. These jackets are like a super cool item for anyone to be seen wearing in the Point. Everybody wants one but few are able to earn one like Sharron did. She had ordered hers in an extra small because she planned to surprise her little brother and give it to him as a gift. She died before she could pick up the jacket.

The crowd gathered for Uncle Patrick's funeral includes cousins, distant relatives and Point people of all ages. Some had met regularly with Uncle Pat in his tiny kitchen where he kept a .45 taped under the table and a rifle tucked between the fridge and counter. The people who knew which side of that kitchen table to stay clear of, coming to pay their respects. The funeral director thinks his contempt is keeping him safe, holding everyone back like a safety rail at the zoo. He doesn't realize it is only respect for my Uncle Pat that is preventing someone from setting him straight. For the moment.

"I want to punch something," announces my cousin Bruce. For a moment he looks the way he did back in grade school, when one of the French schools would invade our schoolyard and a mini-war would break out. Bruce would sometimes get his hands on a baseball bat or a chain and one of the older kids would have to take it away from him. It was the way he grieved. Bruce was looking for a reason to punch something. And the funeral director doesn't realize he is in danger of becoming the reason.

Or the something.

Sheila, Pearl, Dennis and Bruce—Uncle Pat's four kids—couldn't afford an organist. I told them that nobody wants to listen to shit music like that anyway, so instead we pulled out a cassette tape of the Irish Rovers. That's also why they had asked me to give the eulogy. They don't have the donation for a stranger minister, and they know I'd be insulted if they had even tried to offer me a few bucks.

"We don't need some cocksucker saying any bullshit," said Sheila, Uncle Pat's oldest daughter. "You know all the fancy words to say, anyway," she explained. "And we know you love him and will say all the right stuff."

Ever since I had started at Dawson, I'm now considered the family genius. Not only had I graduated from high school, I was also maybe going to eventually get a college certificate. My cousins would have thought I was just being modest, or worse, showing off, if I had tried explaining to them that anyone who could breathe and shit right could earn a certificate from Dawson. So what could I say? They all knew about my ordination and, at this point it was too late to try and explain that I had applied for the clergy license as a fucking joke. So I could wipe my ass with it and mail it back to the church.

"I'm honoured," I say to my cousin. She tries to smile and thank me but is suddenly crying. I'm almost surprised when she allows me to pull her in for a hug.

"It's okay, Sheila," I whisper into her hair. "Really, it's okay. You're going to do it, I promise."

I don't know what the hell I'm promising her she'll be able to do but me being a pastor and all, she believes me.

"I know, I know," she says, finally pulling away, wiping her tears with quick angry fingers.

Behind her I can see Annie has arrived and hasn't noticed yet that Uncle Frankie is moving in close behind her, damn it. I'm not going to make it there in time to warn her. As I move towards them as quickly as possible, trying to move around those still standing and looking for seats, I can see he's saying something to her but can only hear what she says in response.

"No," hisses Annie. "Don't!"

It wasn't said particularly loud but the venom and hatred in her voice is undeniable and makes the room come to an immediate stop.

"Don't TOUCH me."

Even Uncle Frankie finally hears it in her voice and takes a step back. Tears are streaming down his face. "I just wanted a hug," he says in a broken voice.

I'm suddenly feeling so cold I shiver.

"Get away from her," I hear myself saying. I'm proud of how calm my voice is.

Before Uncle Frankie can say anything, two of my favourite cousins have suddenly materialized and are moving him towards the exit. David and Scott each have a firm hand on Uncle Frankie's shoulders and aren't giving him a choice. They are practically shoving him out of the room. Scott catches my eye and we exchange a nod. Uncle Frankie doesn't even try to resist.

"I just wanted a hug!" he says as David and Scott murmur something softly to him before shutting the door behind him.

"You okay?" I ask Annie. She doesn't look okay.

"Fine," she says. "I'm fine. I'm going to grab a seat before they're all gone."

As the Irish Rovers finish up their line about the loveliest of all being the unicorn, I move to the front of the room. Pearl smiles at me encouragingly. Bruce looks at his hands.

"Hello," I say, looking out at the crowd. "Thank you for coming."

A few yell back, "You're welcome!" making the room erupt into laughter. The leader of the Irish gang is standing off to the side at the back of the room next to Aunt Olive, Uncle Pat's wife, a hand on her shoulder. I gave them all a few seconds to settle down.

"It seems wrong that my Uncle Pat isn't here today," I say. "After all, everyone who meant something to him—the people who mattered most —are all crowded in this room together right now. You are the people he thought about, fought about, and cared about with such a passion. I know many of you are feeling utterly lost right now. So what are we to do?"

Sheila's sob seemed to rise up to the ceiling and travel across the entire room as I paused to take a breath. We all pretend not to notice Bruce's heaving shoulders.

"How dare God take him from us," I said. "HOW DARE HE!"

The room was suddenly one huge lump of cement. No one moved.

"What could He have been thinking? How could He have allowed someone so important to so many of us here today to actually leave us?"

I look away from the faces all staring back at me, mouths gaping, each wondering if they had heard correctly. Aunt Olive is nodding her head at the back of the room.

"How lost are we without Uncle Pat to tell us what we need to do next? To remind us of what we know and what we can do? Without his faith and utter belief in what each of us can accomplish? These are just a few of the questions I know many of us here today have been asking ourselves," I say.

I wait a few seconds, then, after looking at several people from the crowd in the eye, I start again.

"I asked myself this morning, what would Uncle Pat say? How would he answer those questions we are all facing right now?"

I can feel the room getting smaller.

" 'You are more than you even know,' he would say. 'How dare you think you need anyone to tell you how to be right in this world!' Yes, he'd be some pissed off with many of us here in this room right now, wouldn't he?"

A few start to murmur, but then catch themselves, afraid of missing Uncle Pat's next thoughts.

"Uncle Pat was that friend. The friend who opened the sliding door in his kitchen to anyone who wanted a hot cup of tea with some Carnation Milk, and a couple of Social Tea Biscuits to dunk. He was that friend who would shut his mouth and let you speak if you needed someone to hear what you really needed to say out loud. He was the keeper of secrets."

I realize the crowd is going to let me talk for as long as my lips keep flapping. It was time to wrap things up.

"When I think of Uncle Pat, I think of my favourite song by James Taylor. 'You've Got a Friend.'" I motion to my cousin Pearl, and she presses the Play button. James Taylor's mellow voice and slow guitar start playing.

"When you're down and troubled…"

Some of them probably don't know who James Taylor is and if they did, they would have wanted to smack him around for his long hair and guitar. The "Hippy Jesus" look isn't so big in the Point.

"Only Christ the Lord Himself should look like Jesus," my Nanny would say. "And that one will be riding a 'Peace Train' straight to hell."

Nanny seems to think James Taylor and Cat Stevens are the same person, maybe because they're both in the "singers doomed for Hell" category. I think it's the hair. And the guitars. Nanny thinks anyone who plays the guitar is a drug addict, and a man with long hair is a man who is afraid to work.

"And wants to be a woman."

As James Taylor wraps it up, I notice the funeral director is back. He has taken his suit jacket off. He tries to catch my eye from the chapel's doorway, signalling for me to hurry things along. I turn my back and walk over to Uncle Pat's coffin.

It's time to leave.

If there's something almost as good as a Point funeral it might be a Point wedding. Not only do you get to see everyone who matters in your life at that moment all piled into the same room, you get to be drunk so everyone becomes less annoying and more fun than usual. Like some of those cousins who can get on your nerves 'cause they not only talk too much but are also boring as hell and need giddy-up noises to spur them along when they get too long-winded with one of their favourite stories that were already shitty and boring the first five times they told it. There's also the ones who are usually too quick to start a fist fight over some insult they decide was directed at them from someone being uppity. Even they are usually more calm and less likely to start any fights, at least for the first three hours, 'cause they're all dressed up in their best stuff. No one wants to get runs or holes in their pantyhose over some girl looking at their man a certain way, or get their glued-on nails ripped off and lost forever on a dance floor. Those suckers don't come cheap. It's really a great way to catch up with just about everybody you know and pay your respects and eat some of the best food and laugh your head off for hours non-stop. I always enjoy hanging out with my cousin Elva. She's the best dancer I know on the planet. I always say she should go on *American Bandstand* or wherever it is that good dancers go as she could teach anybody, anytime, how to be a better dancer. She's really generous about it, too, encouraging you as she gently corrects you, saying, "Move it a bit more like this," and "You got this, girl!" as she shows you how to do the Locomotion and look cool while you're doing it. Maybe Elva makes it look easy because she also happens to be gorgeous?

I always look forward to the pigs in a blanket, too. In the Point, instead of sausages wrapped up in a thin layer of dough, we make them more like hot dogs in a big sleeping bag. I mean, come on, everyone prefers the blanket part over the piggy part, anyway. Within a few hours everyone has orange fingers from the Cheezies, bloated guts from the beer, or black lips and teeth from the cheap red wine. Except for those who have been drinking Molson X all night, and running to the bathroom every ten minutes to prove it. That's where the grass is, anyway, so you can't always tell who is going for a smoke and who is going to take a leak. The wedding cake is always great, too. Piled high with icing and small silver balls that never taste as good as you expect them to, but are still fun to bite down on for some reason. Then the bride will tell everyone to line up for her flower toss and will let us know, before she tosses it, if it's a rental that has to go back (so you can only hold it for the rest of the night, and no pulling any of the flowers out) or if it's a keeper, which we all know means you can dive at the girl who catches it and rip it out of her hands if you can, even if it means the bouquet ends up in ten different pieces among the ten fastest and strongest girls in the room. I always pretend I'm going to go for it but don't really want to catch it. Not that I don't want to get married one day. I do. But I don't want any of these now drunken bitches to put me in a bad mood by trying to grab anything out of my hands if I do catch it. I think it looks really low-rent to get into a fight at a wedding, even if the other person was practically begging for it. So I do try to avoid it most of the time.

I didn't bring Jack with me to the funeral. Besides the fact that I'm thinking of taking a break from Jack, I'm not sure how he'd do with that group and worry he might get his ass kicked for saying something stupid. He actually says shit like, "Smoking weed is illegal, and anyone who smokes is stupid and probably has a death wish." I tell him saying something like that to one of my cousins would suggest he has his own death wish, and he laughs like I'm the funniest person on the planet.

"I'm not kidding," I say. "You can't say stuff like that. It's rude and would really embarrass me if you ever did!"

"How can speaking the truth ever be defined as rude or embarrassing?" says Jack. I'm starting to see the cracks. So he's not perfect. He honestly believes if it's true, it's okay to say. Out loud. No matter what.

"If I were to say I think you're a social retard, wouldn't that be rude?" I ask. I want to punch him when he just laughs.

"Socially retarded? I'll wear that accusation with pride!"

He's grinning like a fool now, waiting and ready to mock whatever comes out of my mouth next.

"Come on," he's now openly encouraging me, "keep going!"

See what I'm dealing with here? Sure, Jack is smart. But also an idiot at the same time. There was no way I could take him to the funeral. I'd find his limp body in the bathroom curled up in a ball, with his beautiful white teeth lying next to him. I wouldn't like him as much without his teeth.

"I have a wedding to go to next Thursday," I tell him.

"Next Thursday? Who has a wedding on a weekday?"

"Uh, my cousin does, that's who."

"Seriously, where will you be going that you don't want to tell me?"

It's hard to try and explain the thinking behind a weekday wedding to someone like Jack.

"Don't worry, you don't have to come," I say.

I admit it worries me a bit when Jack doesn't push it. If he really thinks I'm lying about a wedding, why doesn't he push for the truth?

"I don't understand why you don't like my sisters," I say. I wonder if he can tell somehow that most of them don't like him. Ruth thinks he's an arrogant know-it-all. Annie hasn't said anything too critical but after I found a letter in his top drawer from a girl at his part-time job, saying how much she loves him and how alive her body feels when he's around her and how she can't help but think about him all the time, Annie told me to think about breaking off with him. I was shocked.

"She wrote that letter, he didn't!" I said. How could I blame him for being such an amazing guy that another girl wrote him a love letter? I know he's amazing, that's why I'm with him. Of course other girls want to get with him.

"Has any guy written you a letter, any kind of letter, since you've started dating Jack? Or even just hit on you?"

"Of course not!" Why in hell would a guy do that?

"Bingo," says Annie. I know she thinks she's made some critical point.

"And why did he keep that letter and hide it away in his drawer?"

Of course, I can't ask him about that. He might not like me rummaging through his stuff.

Now that Annie has left for the army as part of her training to become a nurse, Mom and Dad have been packing up, saying this time they're going to leave the province for real. At first, I didn't really believe them, thinking it was just more talk again. Every once in a while the Anglos in Montreal get all worked up, threatening to leave because of Bill 101.

"It promotes the French language by denying the rights of the English!" says Dad.

Dad says Bill 101 means soon you won't be able to speak English at work anymore, even with other Anglos, and no more English signs allowed unless they're half the size of French signs.

"The goddamn language police are now going into shops with measuring tapes," says Nanny. "If the English part isn't half the size of the Frenchie part, they rip down the signs!"

"All the educated and working English are going to leave," says Uncle Michael, "and the only Anglos left behind will be all the welfare bums. Quebec can keep them!"

But Mom says Uncle Mike is just an idiot.

"He's never held down a job his whole life so I guess he's one of the ones who will be staying."

Mom keeps saying she doesn't know what to do about her job with the clinic.

"I'll never be able to make even close to what they're paying me," she says to Dad when he starts bugging her about leaving again. Mom is fluently bilingual. She can stay and work in Quebec. Her French accent is so good, my sisters and I like to irritate each other by asking our mom to say the names of the French metro stations.

"Mom, what's that one that sounds like a lion is growling or something, and starts with an L?"

And Mom always takes the bait.

"Oh, do you mean Lionel-Groulx?"

None of us girls dare to make eye contact.

"Your kids don't speak French," says Dad. "They will always be second-class citizens here."

I like how we become "Mom's kids" whenever we're not doing something right.

Annie can't get a nursing job in Quebec, no matter how high her marks are.

"They're not going to hire me unless I can become more fluent in French," says Annie.

"They're not going to hire you unless you can become a Pepper," says Nanny.

"They're not going to hire you with that kind of an attitude," says Mom.

One of our cousins says they're giving out free cowboy hats to new arrivals in Calgary. Apparently as soon as you arrive they hand you over a huge hat and say, "Howdy partner!" Damn weirdos.

It's starting to look more and more like they're all going to move away from Montreal, though, and I'll be left behind. Alone.

"You have Jack," says Annie on the phone after I call her and cry about everyone leaving me behind. There's some stuff I know I can't tell her over the phone.

"You know Dad wants to move to Calgary because he heard even the bank tellers wear cowboy hats and boots, right?"

Annie laughs. She thinks I'm kidding. But a place like Calgary, where apparently everybody strolls around like they're ready to jump on a horse at any second, is exactly the kind of place our dad would love. I'm not sure why but he's crazy about horses. Annie and I have agreed that whoever gets rich first is gonna buy Dad a horse. Not sure where he'll keep it but he'll figure something out. My cousin Bruce says a lot of people even ride their horses to work in Calgary and I begged him not to tell my dad. Jesus. Between that and the cowboy hats I won't have any chance of being able to talk him and Mom out of going. Every day it seems like another family we know has left the province. I heard that a lot of people are moving to a place called Vancouver, too. I know this can't be true but they're saying it never snows there, just like in China. I'm pretty sure that part is made up but still, it sounds like everyone is moving to either Calgary or Vancouver.

"Everybody gets jobs there as soon as they show up," says my cousin Bruce. "And the pay in Calgary is fucking crazy. They can't even get people to clean toilets or wash dishes anymore 'cause they're all making big bucks now doing stuff with oil rigs."

I'm going to be the only English person left behind. A cartoon in the Montreal *Gazette* asks if the last person to leave the province would please turn off the lights. An article claims over 200,000 Anglos have left already. Where is everybody even getting the money to leave?

On the bus home from work last night I read an ad above the seats across from me. I noticed it because it was in English.

"Alone? Pregnant? Scared? Decisions to Make? Call Birthright! You don't need to go through this alone. We are here to listen and help you. Knowing your options will help you make an informed choice. Free counselling."

Wow. It's like the universe was reading my mind and had posted that sign just for me. Maybe Nanny's right and the Lord really does work in strange ways. Or something like that. A place that's dedicated to the idea that giving birth should be a choice. Wow. I quickly write the phone number down on the back of an envelope in my purse. I never thought I had any options, I thought it was have a baby or kill myself and I don't want to do either. I know Jack doesn't want a baby and to be honest, it's not like I do, either. It would mean dropping out of school and moving back to the Point. How will I take care of a baby if I can't work anymore? How will I take care of me? How will I breathe without Jack in my life? What would it be like to move back to the Point? Pregnant and alone.

"Do you want to have a baby?" I asked him one night. I was three weeks late.

"Maybe one day," said Jack. "You?"

"What would you do if you had to have one right now?"

Jack put the book down and sat up. We'd been lying in bed, both of us doing some reading for our classes the next day.

"A baby right now?" said Jack. "That would be ridiculous and ruin both of our lives, of course. We're both broke students who haven't even begun our lives. Why would we do anything that would create such a major roadblock, possibly derailing our futures and definitely ending our relationship?"

Ending our relationship?

"Why would that end our relationship?" I ask.

I really want to know. I'm thinking a baby could make us closer. I already know it would be beautiful and smart and I would love it so much it would hurt to even look at it. If it is a boy I'd name him Christopher and then call him Chris for short. And if a girl I'd name her Jennifer, and call her Jenn.

"A pregnancy right now would end our relationship as I'd see it as a violation of my trust and faith in you to keep us both protected from something so terrible happening, of course," says Jack with a frown. "To be honest, I just wouldn't be able to love you as much if you could hurt me—hurt us—like that."

Jack said something one time about how when you have eliminated the impossible, whatever remains, however improbable, must be the truth. When I acted super impressed he quickly told me it wasn't his idea.

"But it's something I completely embrace, of course."

Maybe if he hadn't added that "of course" at the end I wouldn't have felt my brain suddenly calling bullshit. But this was Jack, so I had to try. I asked him at what point, though, can you really know that you have in fact "eliminated the impossible"? It made me suddenly recall another equally short-lived debate we had had one time, not long after we had first started dating. I had said I hoped to be able to get a degree so I could get a good job one day and Jack had said going to college or university isn't about getting a job.

"It's about gaining knowledge for its own sake."

It was so soon after we had started dating I didn't say what I really wanted to. That it was obvious he's never had to worry about getting a job.

I decide to wait until Jack's at school to call Birthright.

"Have you confirmed a pregnancy with a test yet?" asked the person on the other end of the line. They sound kind, and like they really do care. It makes me feel weepy.

"No, but I'm feeling sick in the morning, like I could throw up, and my period is almost six weeks late and I'm never late."

"When can you come in?" she asks. "Let's take this one step at a time and, first things first, you need to have a pregnancy test. We'll provide that for you for free."

A pregnancy test? It will be the first test I ever pray to God to help me fail.

When I show up the next morning it makes sense that the Birthright office is in the back of a church. I've been so hard on the church these past few years, thinking it's too judgmental and harsh and takes advantage of people like Nanny, who gives way too much of her small monthly cheque each Sunday.

"Nanny, God wouldn't want you to give that much, really!"

"The Lord has always provided for me," says Nanny. "What I give to the church in return is a pittance."

Nanny rations herself at the end of each month to drinking her tea black and her bread dry once her cash runs out. She also doesn't take the bus to church the last Sunday of each month, instead making the 40-minute walk, both ways, in rain, snow or muggy heat. She says she isn't the only one to fast or make some small sacrifices every once in a while, all in praise of the Lord.

Standing here now, outside the church downtown and about to go in and get some free help with this pregnancy, makes me feel a little ashamed for being so cynical about God in general, and Nanny's church in particular.

They've told me to check in upstairs and I easily find an office with a Birthright sign on the door. I knock and then open the door and see a young woman sitting behind a desk. She looks up at me.

"Kathy?"

I smile and nod and then she hands me a clipboard and pen.

"We'd like you to sign in, please. If you don't mind."

I don't mind. I scribble "D. Barry" and hand it back. It doesn't seem to bother her that I've signed a different name from the one I used on the phone.

"You can go right in," she says and nods towards another door to her right.

"Good morning!" says the young, good-looking guy sitting behind yet another desk. "Please," he says with a friendly smile, "have a seat."

As I sit down I have a short coughing fit. I'm nervous.

"Would you like some water?" He's standing now, ready to dash off and fetch me a drink.

"No, no," I say and smile back at him. "Just nerves. I'm fine."

He sits back down.

"So, I'm Derek. How can I help you, Ms….?"

"You can call me Dee," I say. "Uh, are you a doctor?"

He looks startled. Like I've asked him something a little off.

"Oh, no, no," he says. "Just a volunteer. Uh, we all are. Volunteers."

"Right. That's nice. I think I was expecting a pregnancy test today? They said it was free. On the phone?"

"Yes, right, of course!" says Cute Guy. I've already forgotten his name. "But first let me tell you about our services, okay?"

I nod my head.

"We offer three services. First, we offer friendship!"

I just smile. I know it would be rude to say I don't want any new friends.

"We also offer a free pregnancy test and third, we support the right of every pregnant woman to give birth and the right of every child to be born. Let's put it this way—we are sharing God's love through our actions and in our experience. You'll find the love of Jesus and a renewed sense of hope and faith through our work here with you."

Uh, and where exactly is the abortion option?

He stands up and waves for me to follow him over to a closet door. After he opens it I can see rows and rows of small glass test tubes standing up in small metal trays, and piles of small white packages.

"See this?" he says. He's holding up one of the metal trays of test tubes. "We'll take a urine sample from you today and then call you with the results. If your test tube ends up like this one," he has carefully lifted one out of the tray and is holding it up close to my face, "see how it has what looks like a small donut near the bottom?"

I have no idea what the fuck he is talking about. A small donut? A urine sample? What the hell?

"Sure," I say, trying to buy some time. But do I really want to give a urine sample? How can I pee in a tall skinny test tube without peeing all over myself? Am I really going to let Cute Guy see my pee?

"Here," he says, handing me a plastic cup with a lid. "Take it into the washroom and after you're done just leave it with Janice at the desk. But before you go, just let me fill in a small bit of paperwork first, all right?"

Back at his desk he's holding a form and a pen.

"When was your last period? Do you remember the exact date?"

I'm waiting for the part about whether Jesus is my close and personal saviour and wondering what the hell I'll say when we get there. Bible thumpers aren't too happy about people having sex, lots of sex, before they're married and shit. I wonder if Cute Guy is going to assume maybe I was forced to get pregnant? Or will he think I'm just dumb and don't know how this shit works?

"How long have you been sexually active?" he asks.

Wow. Great way around it, right? Maybe I'm supposed to burst into tears at this point and swear I did it just once—just that one time—and now I'm worried I might be pregnant.

"Not that long," I say. I mean, Jesus Christ, what the hell was I supposed to say? What's the right answer to that? Oh, not so long, promise. Or, I've been fucking for years now. Sex is great, right?

When I finally get out of there I'm surprised I was able to pee on command. Why do they have the guy doing the interviews and asking the questions, and the girl directing traffic? He should switch places with her. I had wanted to ask about where I'd be able to get the abortion if the test comes back saying I'm pregnant, which I'm pretty sure it will. I hate having to continue to wait. I know the longer this takes the harder it will be. Mom helps Point girls get their abortions after they have nowhere else to turn, after their parents say they're against them killing the baby. She's had to smuggle a few over the border into the States because they're so young she couldn't find a doctor willing to do the procedure in Canada without a signature from their parents.

"Damn idiots," said Mom. "Forcing babies to have babies."

I know Mom won't help me. I'm not a baby. I'm almost 18 and should have known better. Should never have gotten caught like this. I'm so embarrassed. Almost more embarrassed than I am scared. I've heard Mom talking about some doctor like she worships the ground he walks on. Apparently he even sent a letter to the Prime Minister, bragging he'd already done over five thousand abortions, detailing how he's done them and also promised he has no intentions of stopping. The police kept raiding his clinic and finally even put his ass in jail for more than ten months until he had a heart attack, and then they transferred him to a nursing home or something. Anyway, the fact that he survived a concentration camp and then, instead of just living his life below the radar after getting free of all that, he decided fuck it, and risked losing his career and going to prison for years makes him sound pretty bad-ass. He told the press that if he didn't offer women abortions, some of them would continue to die from trying to do their own abortions on themselves at home. It seems like he's in the newspapers every second day.

"In a case of unwanted or accidental pregnancy, a woman should have the right to choose an abortion, under excellent medical conditions—to protect her life, health and future fertility."

I went back to the church to find out if I had peed a teeny donut in the bottom of that glass tube or not. I admit it took a while but I realized that I'm a fucking idiot, because "Birthright" apparently doesn't mean I'm the one with the right to decide if I give birth.

"You tested positive," Cute Guy said to me.

For a couple of seconds I was thrilled. I thought "tested positive" meant I wasn't pregnant. You know, positive news means no baby. Then when I said, "Thank you!" he looked at me kind of strangely and said, "You wanted to be pregnant?"

Then it hit me right in the gut and I had to take small breaths. I'm pregnant. I'm fucking pregnant. There is a baby, a fucking baby, growing inside of me right now. I don't even remember what I said next to Cute Guy or how I even got home. Just some messy memory of stumbling out of the church and running down the sidewalk until I was so out of breath I had to stop, just to breathe. I'm pregnant.

I call Dr. Morgentaler's clinic and find out that although the clinic believes in the right to women having access to a safe abortion no matter what the law says, what they really mean is that "right" is for women who can also pay $400 or more, depending on how pregnant they are. Oh, and cash only. I felt ashamed and stupid when I cried on the phone and tried explaining to the nurse that I'm a student and don't have that kind of money.

"Maybe the baby's father does? He should help with this as well, of course."

The baby's father? I have been thinking this is a pregnancy, not a baby. Now I have no choice. I know Mom is going to give me a hard time about it and I hate her having to know so much about my life but this has gone on too long. I'm throwing up all the time now and I know this has to happen sooner rather than later. Shit, otherwise I'm going to start thinking of this as a baby, too.

"What does Jack say?" asks Mom. It's the first thing she says after I tell her I'm pregnant and need an abortion.

What does Jack say? Hmmm. What do I want her to think Jack said?

"He says he'll support whatever decision I make."

"And you're sure terminating the pregnancy is what you want?" Mom isn't giving anything away about how she feels. This is an inquisition.

"I don't really have much of a choice, do I? I mean, I'm barely making enough right now to pay my bills and I've still got two more years of school to go. I can't work and go to school if I have a baby, right?"

"You've got it all figured out, don't you?"

Uh oh.

"A pregnancy is an inconvenience for you right now so fuck that, just rip it out."

Jesus Christ.

"No, I'd rather wait a bit longer until I can feel it moving around, maybe even kicking a bit in there and *then* rip it out."

I want to ask her why the fuck does she care, anyway. She's helped so many women and young girls have abortions, what the hell is the difference if she helps one more?

"That's my grandchild," says Mom. Her voice sounds funny so it takes a second for what she said to sink in.

"Your grandchild? That's your grandchild? Are you for real?"

I want my mother to love me, even if just for a few minutes. Just long enough that I can yell how much I hate her, really hate her guts, and then watch her face crumple into hurt. I watch as her eyes get small and her face starts to harden and I remind myself that I do actually need her help. I have no fucking clue how to make this happen. I know it's not as easy as simply showing up at one of the city hospitals and making a special request. And the clinic in the Point doesn't do abortions so I don't know of anyone else to go to.

"I'm disappointed you'd put a man before a baby," says Mom.

I have no fucking clue what she means by that but she's calm again and not talking anymore about me killing her grandchild, so I just give a vague nod and try to look sad instead of enraged. Mom has always dealt much better with sadness than anger. But everything in me wishes I could afford to tell her to fuck off.

Chapter Eight

My sister Ruth has graduated from ripping the wings off flies to now trapping them in a plastic bag. Seriously, I'm not kidding. Apparently they sell these things—some kind of a bag—at the hardware store. You hang it up anywhere you want and it will attract flies for miles and miles around. I think Ruth said it contains some kind of sugar or sweet stuff that the flies can smell from 25 miles away.

"Why do you want to attract flies from other neighbourhoods?" I ask her, though I already know the answer. "Don't you have enough of the damn things right here hanging around and flying about?"

Ruth has been luring flies to her death traps for years now. It used to be good enough to simply remove their wings and turn them into something else. But now she actually just wants them dead. She could teach a course at Dawson about flies and not just how to kill them. Seriously, she's a damn expert on the disgusting things.

"House flies can carry over a hundred different pathogens, including typhoid, cholera, tuberculosis and anthrax," says Ruth.

Ever since she started that nursing program she uses fancy words like "pathogen" and "sterile" all the time, throwing them around like they're nothing.

"And flies are getting smarter, too," explains Ruth. "Some species have even become immune now to insecticides."

Okay, I admit it. That was a bit interesting. How the hell do flies become immune to something? And becoming smarter? Flies?

"How did that happen?"

"Oh, people think they're called the 'common' housefly like they're just so common, they're dumb or something," says Ruth. "But in this case, 'common' just means there are a lot of them as they're found all over the world. These bastards shit and vomit on your food in countries just about everywhere!"

Ruth says when you see them rubbing their hands together like they do, as if in glee, they are in fact doing exactly that. Apparently those flies are in their damn glory.

"They usually fuck only once and then save the sperm for later," says Ruth.

Ruth reads my face and adds, "No, seriously, I'm not kidding. They really do that! They need to find something dead to lay their eggs on for them to hatch properly. That's why they look for dead animals or garbage to drop their eggs on."

But saving the sperm for later? I mean, who knew that flies even have sperm? What's the matter with me? Why did I think only guys have sperm? Then again, what the hell did I think a sperm whale is? But I just can't wrap my head about saving the sperm for later. No wonder some people are paranoid about getting pregnant from a public toilet seat.

Ruth explains how small flies aren't necessarily babies or even young adults. They're just the runts of the litter, the ones that didn't get enough dead stuff to eat while they were babies.

"Not only do they have to find something dead to give birth to their babies on," says Ruth, "if they don't get enough to feed off when they're in the larval stage, they'll be stunted later."

Like I said, she could teach a damn college course about this shit.

"Uh, you know how weird this all makes you sound, right?"

"Why?" says Ruth. "The study of flies is where all the theories come from about oxidative molecular damage making us get older. Without it, we might even live forever. Hell, researchers have learned so much from studying flies they might find a way to help us live twice as long as we live now, just from the simple housefly."

I wonder why she's a serial killer of flies, then? I mean, if those little fuckers help us so much, might even one day give us the secret to living forever, why kill them?

"Why are you drowning flies?" I ask.

"Well, here's the thing," says Ruth. "It can hold up to 500 flies. If you trap a lot of babies it can hold even more, since they're smaller. They're too stupid to get out. They swim around a bit and then they drown. Mind you, after a while that bag starts to stink to high heaven!"

Ruth seems to think I've asked why she picked one method for killing flies over the other, rather than why she's made it her holy mission to execute as many flies as possible. And holy shit, she's done her research.

"Uh, what do you do with the bags when you're done with them?" I have to ask.

"You mean when they're so stuffed full that even the tiniest gnat wouldn't be able to work its way in there?" says Ruth.

Yeah, I've made her day. Ruth lives for the follow-up questions when she's in the middle of a favourite story. But I'm asking her because I actually want to know.

"How do you get rid of it afterwards? What do you do with it?"

My head is quickly filling with all kinds of horror scenarios of what happens with that bag and I know the only way to stop it from filling with more is to simply find out the truth. Does she burn it? Throw it into the garbage? Bury it? Cast a magical spell?

"Don't worry about it," says Ruth.

Don't get me wrong—even if she's a fly serial killer, I've learned to appreciate Ruth over the years in ways I didn't when we were younger, back when she belonged to Nanny. Back then she had Nanny's voice, too, which was a special kind of terrible coming out of a kid's face. You gotta be above a certain age and be wearing a hat with plastic flowers glued to it in order to be able to pull off a "Praise the Lord!" and "That is just the Devil's work!" and not sound like a fucking insane person. It was Annie who explained it all to me one day, forcing me to give Ruth a bit of a break for sounding like a bossy old lady half the time.

"You can't hold it too much against her," said Annie. "It's not her fault that Mom gave her to Nanny to try and keep Dad close and be sure to have at least one of us kids fed all the time and able to wear socks and underwear every single day."

It's like Annie could tell those were the three things I hated most about Ruth. She had socks, underwear and food every single day.

"It's not like she asked to, either. I'm sure she would've preferred to stay here with us girls and be able to watch *Batman and Robin* on Sundays, instead of wearing out her knees saying thanks to baby Jesus and his dad, God, for all the good food they were providing for her over at Nanny's place."

I thought about it on and off for a while, trying to decide if I would have given up my sisters and Mom just to have some socks, underwear and supper every single day, guaranteed. Ruth liked to come over whenever she had a Fudgsicle or new pair of shoes to show off.

"Wanna lick?" she'd ask, then give a mean laugh and pull it away just as your tongue started to stretch out and almost reach it. I can't count how many times she managed to fool us with that one. She was smart, though, as every once in a while she'd let you get in a good lick and then you'd be thinking she was going to be nice like that forever. Then next time she'd be suddenly pulling it away again, laughing that she didn't want our ugly germs all over her food. One time I smacked it out of her hand by mistake and even I made a sound of shock and horror right along with her when it suddenly hit the sidewalk. Of course it was only made about a million times worse when Nanny happened to open the door at the very second that damn Fudgsicle was about to hit the dirty curb. Her gasp was so loud no one heard mine as we all watched it, like it was happening in slow motion, tumble around like it was trying to get as filthy and banged up as possible. Nanny instantly looked at me and demanded to know what had happened. She was breathing so hard her words came out almost breathless.

"What did you DO?" Her face was so frozen in ugliness I couldn't even reply right away. And then Ruth answered her instead.

"Oh darn it, Nanny, I'm a clumsy fool, I'm sorry. I know I just wasted God's creation and spilled your hard-earned ten cents all over the filthy sidewalk and I promise I will make it up to you and Him both." Then she hung her head in shame.

Nanny and I were both speechless for a second.

"Well then, no point in crying over spilt milk," said Nanny. "Maybe it's for the best as it won't be spoiling your appetite for dinner."

Then after a curt nod to me, "Come along, Ruth, we best be getting home before that rump roast burns up in the oven."

Yeah. I tried not to hate them both at that moment. Ruth for the sliced beef I knew she'd be having for dinner as soon as she got back to

Nanny's. And Nanny for assuming I must have been involved somehow, even if she was right, for someone's sacred food falling onto the ground.

As they walked away, Ruth sneaked a peek at me behind Nanny's back and gave me a small grin. I gave her the finger. Spoiled bitch.

A few years later, after our cousin Bruce was born and Nanny decided she wanted an upgrade, Ruth came back to live with us full-time. She was always trying to make us move over and make some room for her but it was too late for her to act like the oldest. That was Annie's job now. Ruth could try and boss us around as much as she wanted. No one would listen. Eventually we had to start sharing our underwear and socks days with her as well. I realized one day that Ruth knows a lot of our family secrets. She's real good at keeping secrets, too. Sometimes I try to do a trade with her. You know, I'll tell her something if she'll tell me something.

"You don't know anything I don't already know," says Ruth. "And if you do, it's not worth knowing."

She's good. She's hoping I'll suddenly start spilling just to try and prove her wrong. But I'm not that dumb. She tries a different approach. One she's learned from Nanny. Instead of talking direct, she tells a story and it's up to you to find it buried among the details. Problem is, Ruth is a really good storyteller. I get caught up in all of the little, really interesting details and then forget to look for the "truths."

"Did you know you have to think like the rat?" says Ruth.

What the fuck does that mean?

"No, really," says Ruth. "It's true. You have to think like the rat. They're creatures of habit. They establish trackways through a house, following the same paths each day, in and out, to food and to rest. I mean, think about it. When you hear a rat moving around in the walls it's never a new part of the wall, right? Nope. It's always close to the same area you heard it the night before. And did you know a rat has amazing swimming ability?"

"Uh, who teaches them how to swim?" It's all I got. What would you have asked or said to her at that moment?

"Who teaches anything how to swim," says Ruth. "They just get tossed into the sewer and it's sink or swim."

I wonder if I can change the story. Have Ruth maybe tell me about something else I've been wondering about.

"Did Nanny ever tell you about that girl who cried herself to death? A girl who was so sad and was so sure she didn't want to live anymore she just cried and cried and finally died. Do you think that's even possible? I mean, maybe Nanny just made it up, right? You know, to teach me something? Or do you think it's true?"

I hate that Ruth will know this is something I've been wondering about for years. I've been sad for that girl for a long time.

"I know that story, too," says Ruth. "She didn't die right away, though, and it wasn't because of sadness that she was crying. She was afraid."

Oh man. Maybe we should go back to the rats doing their routine walks in the wall right beside my bed each night instead?

"And she cried for days. She didn't actually think it would kill her, though. That was an unexpected bonus."

Ruth is the most loyal human being I know on the planet once she decides you're part of her inner circle. I mean, with Ruth that is a pretty small circle, made up mostly of just me and our other sisters and Mom and Dad. But once you're in that circle of Ruth's, you don't even have to be loyal back. She will stand by you, have your back, and cross any line in the sand drawn by anybody else once she's decided to be loyal to you. Forever. No matter what. We share that secret weakness together, even if we never speak of it. It's our Achilles heel, something Nanny explained to me one time years ago with a story that made me think, Holy shit! That's what my weakness is; my Achilles heel is the loyalty I have for the people I love.

Nanny has said Achilles was a Greek baby whose mom stuck him, without so much as a diaper on, into a special river when he wasn't even a week old to make him safe from any kind of injury ever, like a superhero. But the only problem was that after she stuck him in she forgot to change the position of her hand and put the part she had first held him by in the water, so that part would also be protected. So that tiny part of his heel, that part that never got stuck into this special Greek river, ended up being his only weak part. It's a great story, just the kind Nanny would know and tell you about, trying to teach some important but hidden message. Nanny is a lot like Jesus. She doesn't just outright tell you shit. Nope. She speaks in parables and stories, hiding the warnings and important truths behind bullshit like wells and fishes and red seas and long hair. Hell, even whores are sometimes the part of the story that important truths are hidden behind. I asked Nanny one time, when I was really young, why Jesus couldn't just be a straight shooter and she told me I should have my filthy mouth washed out with soap. I wanted to tell Nanny that if a mother from the Point had found some kind of special lake or river she could dunk her kid in and make them invincible, she'd be dropping that kid in headfirst, then fishing his wet body out afterwards. Then she'd be taking a dive in herself as well and finally, she'd be telling all the other moms in the neighbourhood about it, too.

Of course, to reveal to Ruth that I know this loyalty thing about her would be just rude. Like telling someone they look like they've gotten soft, or calling them out on any other weakness. You don't tell someone that you've figured out the chink in their armour, their weak spot that can lead to their downfall.

Chapter Nine

I'M NOT SURE IF THEY EXPECT a blow or a snow job but the three old men seated at the long table aren't really looking at me, anyway. They're mostly looking down at the papers in front of them, as if searching for answers they seem to assume I won't have.

"You think you're about eight weeks pregnant, is that correct?"

He is still looking down so it takes me a couple of seconds to realize that, yes, he's talking to me. The three doctors had all mumbled their names when I first shuffled into the room but I was so focused on trying to keep the back flap of my Johnny Shirt closed I didn't retain any of their names. Which is fine; apparently none of them will even be doing the procedure. These guys just get to decide if I should be allowed to have my abortion, but not do it themselves. They could be brothers. Or more likely triplets since they look exactly the same age and have the same facial expressions—bored, boreder, and fucking boredest. They get to decide right now whether I'm dropping out of school, quitting my job, and having a baby, or getting it sucked out by a tube attached to some kind of a special high-tech vacuum machine.

"The procedure itself shouldn't take more than five minutes," explained the doctor at the appointment Mom finally set up for me, the preliminary meeting, last week. He doesn't get to approve the procedure itself, though. He's just the one who gets to describe it and then later perform the procedure if I do get approved. Mom came with me to the appointment. I was secretly relieved that she did, though of course I acted like I didn't care either way. After we arrived at the doctor's office, a receptionist in the crowded waiting room handed me a clipboard with a pen and a form for me to fill out.

"Just let me know if you have any questions," she yelled over once she got back to her desk.

I wondered if all the other women in the room were there for the same thing. Some of them looked too old to have an abortion. A few looked too young. I looked down at the forms and was glad we had arrived early for the appointment. This was going to take a while. I was also glad Mom was with me since the forms didn't seem to throw her off at all. I'd softly read out the questions, in practically a whisper just so the whole room didn't have to know my business, and then she'd tell me what to write. Some of it was easy and obvious of course. Name, age, address, check. Occupation?

"Uh, should I say where I work?" I asked Mom.

"No, put 'full-time' student," she says. "It looks better."

She whispers the next part so low I have to ask her to say it again.

"A student being pregnant is worse. So it's better to write that."

I wonder why being a pregnant student is worse? I'd think being a worker would be worse, no? But I know I can't have this long, whispered conversation with my Mom in the doctor's waiting room so I just write "student" in the box.

Mom is reading over my shoulder and just nods when I fill in the parts that I don't even have to ask for help with. I know the name of my school and can pull out a paper that has its address on it for that section of the form. Then I get to a question that stops me for just a second.

"Why are you here? Please briefly describe what you are here to see the doctor for."

That stumps me for a second. I'm here to see the doctor to see if he can help me get approved for an abortion next week at the hospital. I'm hoping he will be able to get the committee to accept my application for an abortion under the therapeutic clause, and then assuming I do get approved, that he will personally perform the abortion. Mom has told me he's one of the best. Seems like a sad thing to be the best at but what do I know about these things, right? Now I'm worried my answer isn't going to be "brief," as requested, so after hesitating for another few sections, I simply write that I'm here for an abortion. That gets an instant reaction out of my Mom. She forgets to whisper.

"No, not that!" she says and then takes the pen from me and starts to scribble all over the word "abortion" until you no longer can tell what the word used to be. It's now completely covered up.

"Instead, write that you're here for a D and C," says Mom. She's back to whispering again.

"What's a D and C?" I ask her. I thought I was here to ask about an abortion?

"Shh," says Mom. "Just write it."

Then she takes the pen and clipboard from me and writes it herself. "It's a medical procedure to… to clean out your uterus," she whispers.

The receptionist announces my name and stands up for me to follow her. I take the clipboard from Mom and hand it over to the receptionist. Once we're in the examination room she doesn't waste any time.

"Strip off everything from the waist down," she says, then hangs my clipboard up on a nail on the door. "The doctor will be right in."

It feels cold and almost scary to be naked from the waist down and I can't decide whether to sit on the edge of the thin mattress on the examining table, or lie down. Or maybe just wrap the small sheet around my waist and sit on the chair that is close to the bed? Before I can decide, the door is suddenly flung open and the doctor strolls in.

"Why don't you just lie down," he says as he lifts my clipboard off the nail and quickly scans it.

"I thought you were here to consult about an abortion. What's with the D and C?"

I want to kill my mother.

"Uh, yeah, an abortion. Sorry."

The doctor puts down the clipboard and lifts my legs into the stirrups.

"I'm sure you have a lot of questions but let me give you the overview first and then see where we are, okay?"

Damn, I should have written some questions down. Make me look like I'm involved and care.

"It won't be very painful at all. If anything, more like severe menstrual cramps."

I guess his severe menstrual cramps haven't been too bad.

"Your pregnancy is still at the embryo stage which means you'll have the surgical aspiration method, which is the safest and most common at your stage. It just involves inserting a hollow plastic tube attached to a suction machine into your uterus through the cervix."

Jesus. I don't want to listen but I know I need to.

"A local anaesthetic will be injected into your cervix to control any pain before it's dilated."

139

The doctor looks up from between my legs and stares at my face for a few seconds.

"Don't forget. The Therapeutic Abortion Committee doesn't want to give you a problem so help them make it easy. Okay? Got it?"

"Make what easy?"

I know he thinks he's talking to a complete moron as he takes a deep breath before he continues.

"The decision to approve your request for a therapeutic abortion. My understanding is that you will... you'll... that you might do some serious harm to yourself if forced to continue with this pregnancy, right?"

Do serious harm? I wonder how they define "serious harm"? I want to ask if dropping out of college and having to be Kathy from the Point again would count as "serious harm"? Does losing Jack count as serious harm? Does no longer being able to work count as serious harm? I'm not ready to be a mother. I don't want to be a mother. I don't want to be pregnant. I want it to be just me again. I want to only have to worry about me again. I look back at the doctor, but he's no longer looking at me and is engaged with my vagina again; then he suddenly stands up and starts to push on my stomach.

"Wait, so... do I have to actually say that?" I ask him. "To this Abortion Approval Gang?"

He ignores my renaming of the committee. Maybe he doesn't know that I joke when I'm nervous or upset.

"They might expect you to articulate a specific concern about continuing the pregnancy representing potential serious harm to you, or they might ask you nothing and simply stamp your file. My point is, once you get to that stage, make it easy for them. Tell them how much a threat this continued pregnancy presents to your mental well-being."

I don't know why this is hard for any of *them* and I know the doctor is growing impatient with the stupid girl lying on the table before him. I wish I could be that girl Nanny told me about years ago, the one who cried to death. I know this doctor wouldn't hate me as much if I could only cry. But I can't. It's impossible. I can barely blink, never mind force out some tears to make everybody happy.

"After the procedure it's important that you stay out of hot baths for a little while as it can induce further bleeding," he says. "And make sure you get this filled as soon as you leave here."

He's handing me a paper and I see it's a prescription for birth control pills. I don't know whether it will make me look worse or better to tell him I've been on the pill for almost a year.

"Any questions?"

He isn't looking at me anymore. He's done.

"No? Good. You can get dressed now."

I actually now have about a million questions but I don't know how to ask most of them. Will the baby feel any… pain? Or do we share the pain meds they'll be giving to me? Will I ever be able to get pregnant again one day in the future? How many days will I bleed for afterwards? Can I go back to school and work right away?

Will Jack have to sign anything?

I've been afraid to ask about that one the most.

"What would you say if I told you I'm pretty sure I'm pregnant?" I had finally blurted it out to Jack one night after we had been through a couple of good days. Like when we had first met, when I knew he loved me for sure, and would always want to be together forever. No matter what.

"What would I say if you told me that you're pretty sure you're pregnant?"

I hate it when he does that. Repeats my question before finally answering it. Buying some time is what I suspect.

"I'd say I'm pretty sure I'm not the father," says Jack, "since I *know* how careful I've been."

The crushing sensation in the middle of my chest is immediate and overwhelming. I can't even take a breath to tell Jack that I think I'm having a heart attack and he needs to call 911. It takes me a second or two before I can breathe or even whisper, but just as I'm about to speak, Jack leaves the room.

"See ya later," he says over his shoulder as he shuts the apartment door.

I suddenly found myself sitting on the floor and took some deep breaths. Maybe it would just be easier this way? Or maybe I just made that all up in my head? I get up off the floor and look out the window. I can't see him anymore. He had moved on so fast.

My attention snaps back to the office.

"I'll meet you at the reception desk in a few minutes," says the doctor. He's done explaining the abortion procedure. Now it's time for me to get all the necessary paperwork from his receptionist.

"One quick question?" I say before he can leave the room. He stops and turns around.

"When?" I ask. "When will I have this... done?"

"My nurse will give you the exact date and address. Don't worry," he says with a smile. "I promise we're going to take great care of you. She'll also give you an appointment to come back and see me the day after, and then six weeks after that for follow-up care."

I wonder what the follow-up care will be? The baby will be gone, right?

Less than a week later, I'm standing before the three doctors seated behind a long table, file folders and papers scattered in front of them. I wonder for a second what my file might say if I were able to somehow sneak a peek at it. One of the old guys clears his throat and I know it's time.

"Miss Dobson, you know why you're here today?"

I seriously have to fight back all the smart-ass comments that instantly come to mind. Thank god there's no one else from the Point in the room, or even worse, one of my sisters. I wouldn't have been able to help myself. I'd have played to them until one of these old guys would have finally kicked me out of the room. Then again, come to think of it, killing babies is the one thing you probably can't make a joke about with people from the Point. Maybe an uncle too quick with his hands, or a grandpa who likes to give wet kisses to a four-year-old? Hilarious. We can joke about perverts in the family, hungry children without any clean underwear or socks to wear, and moms who look funny the way they always seem to flinch or duck when their husband or ex strolls into the room. But killing babies? Before they've even had a chance to be born? There is nothing lower than that. Unless you were under the age of, say, ten, and begged your dad, uncle, cousin, the stranger in the Wellington tunnel, or whoever, to stop, and had to be hospitalized afterwards from putting up such a great fight that you're going to need some emergency surgery to close up all those wounds he opened all over your tiny body as your small fists pounded on him and he beat the shit out of you in anger when you didn't just lie back and take it. Otherwise, you, my friend, are a baby killer and will be going straight to hell one day. But before you do? The people around you will be there to remind and hate you, every single day for the rest of your life for what you did. Oh, they might not say it to your face so much after the first year or so has passed. But they will continue to talk about you behind your back. For years.

"Imagine? How could she be so damn selfish?"

"Does she have any idea what they did to kill that baby even before they ripped it out of her by its tiny arms and tiny legs and perfectly formed baby head? You know they can actually already think around the seven-week mark, right? Form memories at eight weeks."

Yeah, and learn a fucking second language at nine weeks.

"She is a piece of shit."

"No one will ever marry that slut now. Whore."

"What a cunt!"

"She'd rather kill her baby than have to drop out of school or lose a *man*? What a piece of work."

That last one was said by my mother. She warned me to never speak of any of this with my dad. Or her, ever again.

"He'd never forgive you. That's his grandchild, too. I doubt he'd ever even speak to you again."

The doctors sitting behind the long table seem done. They're still waiting for my reply. Finally.

"I'm here to... end it."

They look over at each other, shuffle the pile of papers in front of them one last time, then finally the one on the far end looks at me and speaks.

"Just go through the door on your left."

A nurse tells me to wiggle down a bit more so my butt can be closer to the edge of the bed. The room seems completely filled with busy medical people. I think the doctor is the one with the small cap tied around his head, but I'm still not a hundred percent sure. He's sitting on what looks like a low, rolling bar stool. He doesn't look up as I try to wiggle to the end while keeping my legs as closed shut as possible. I'm naked from the waist down and I don't want to flash the whole room. Another nurse comes over and leans down close to my face.

"Hi Kathy, I'm Diana and I'll be your nurse today. The doctor is going to inject your cervix in a minute with a drug that will numb it from the pain. We'll be done real soon, though, promise!" Then she smiles and gives my hand a gentle squeeze. She's being so nice it makes me feel weak. The guy on the rolling bar stool is suddenly now rolled over to the end of the bed and at perfect eye level with my knees. He pulls on them gently, prying them apart.

"Come on," he says. "Open up." Then lowers his seat even further. Now he's at eye level with my crotch.

Everything suddenly now seems to move forward quickly as a loud machine drowns out every other sound in the room. I can feel the doctor poking around down below and I try to ignore him and focus on something else. Diana the nurse leans down again close to my face.

"Don't be afraid, sweetie. It'll all be over before you know it. Right now the doctor is inserting the tube; I promise that's the worst of it."

I'm concentrating on taking deep breaths now. That tube is hurting like hell. I'm wondering if the doctor is maybe shoving it up the wrong spot as it feels like whatever he's pushing on is not going to let that tube in. It hurts. I don't want to cry but my eyes are watering and now the nurse is making sympathetic noises that make me want to tell her not to worry about me, I'll be fine. But I'm afraid I'll make crying sounds if I try to talk so I just try to smile at her. She reaches over and takes my other hand and is now holding both of them tightly in her hands.

"Almost done," she says. "Almost done."

Then she starts to make shushing sounds and leans in even closer and puts her arm around my right shoulder.

"It's okay, hush, hush. It's okay."

I feel embarrassed now and want to tell her it's not me making that high-pitched cry. It must be some other girl in a nearby room. But I need to concentrate on not having my insides turned inside out by that loud machine that is sucking my uterus out through the skinny straw the doctor has shoved up me.

When the machine suddenly stops there's no warning. One minute it was so loud I could barely make out what the nurse was whispering into my ear as she hugged me so tightly I couldn't take a deep breath, and the next second the entire room was suddenly so quiet, you could hear the sound of papers being crinkled from across the room.

"There!" says the doctor as he stands up from his bar stool.

"That wasn't so bad now, was it?" He pulls off his gloves and tosses them on a small table next to him and walks away.

Nurse Diana gently pushes me back down when I try to sit up.

"Just a sec, sweetie," she says. "We just need to get you all fixed up down there."

Another nurse is pulling my underwear on up over my legs with what feels like a huge pad attached. As she gets close to the top of my legs I lift up my butt and suddenly I'm wearing a huge diaper. It feels weird and bulky between my legs, making it impossible for me to close them fully. After standing up, Nurse Diana tells me to move slowly. I know I'm doing more of a waddle than a walk, thanks to the king-sized diaper. It feels like a little bit of my insides is gushing out with every step I take.

"Don't worry," says Nurse Diana. "It's totally normal."

How does she know?

"You'll rest for about an hour in the recovery room," she says as she guides me out of the room and into a hallway, "and then you can leave. Who is here to bring you home?"

"My boyfriend," I say. "He's waiting outside. In the small park across the street. He's wearing a hat."

Damn it. I hope I haven't given too many details. Sometimes that can give a lie away. I should have just stuck to the basics. She had simply asked "who?" Why the hell did I tell her all that stuff about being across the street and the park?

"What's his name, sweetie?"

Shit.

"Uh, why?"

She stops walking and looks at me with surprise on her face.

I start to tell her that I'm sorry for being weird and that his name is Jack but she's calling for help and then pushing me into a wheelchair after someone comes rushing down the hall pushing one and delivers it right in front of me.

"I don't need a chair," I say, and then see the thin trail of blood behind me, now also forming a small puddle at my feet. My thighs feel wet now. I'm surprised anything has made it past my diaper. It still feels like I've got a small mattress squeezed between my legs.

"How…?"

"No worries, sweetie, just sit."

With that she pressed firmly on my shoulders, forcing me to sit down in the chair. I want to tell her it's okay, that if anything it makes me feel better to be bleeding. But I'm just too tired to talk. I feel my eyes close and decide I'll tell her later, after I wake up.

Chapter Ten

ONE OF THE THINGS I FIND WEIRD about Dawson that I recently learned is that they keep a bunch of mice and rats locked up in a laboratory as prisoners in the basement. I mean, sure, it's not cats and dogs, or cows and children, or anything, but still. When I first heard about it from Mark, my prof that teaches the Psychology of Human Sexual Behaviour class, I thought he was messing with me. Like it was his rich guy way of flirting, or something. Yeah, I know, but seriously it could easily have been that. I've met a lot of guys outside of the Point now at Dawson and I can always tell which ones are from neighbourhoods like the Point or Verdun or even LaSalle, and which ones are from the more upscale neighbourhoods. It's all about the weird way they flirt. Instead of giving you compliments about how you look or showing off how strong they are or what a great job they have, they do stuff like ask you questions. What's your favourite music? What do you like to eat? Who are you reading right now? See what I mean. Weird, eh?

"So, what exactly do you do with these prisoners?" I asked, not sure yet how to react to such a strange fact, such a freaky piece of information. Slaves in the school's damn basement? Not exactly small talk, right?

"Oh, we experiment on them," said Mark.

"Experiment?" I wasn't sure if that deserved a fake laugh or a frown. "What do you mean?"

"We have dozens of them in the lab each year," said Mark with a straight face. "They're ideal subjects for psychology experiments."

That didn't sound even remotely hot to me.

"Uh, what kinds of experiments?"

I wanted to look over my shoulder to see if any of the other students had shown up to class yet. Damn my eagerness to be on time for this guy's class. Suddenly I wasn't so keen to be alone with him anymore.

"Rats make ideal subjects because their behavioral characteristics actually closely resemble humans' in numerous ways. All kinds of symptoms of the human condition can be replicated in rats under controlled experiments."

I guess my mouth must have been hanging open a bit.

"Seriously," he added with a bit of a laugh. "Rats have served as an important animal model for all kinds of research projects in psychology. And, of course, biomedical science as well."

Well, fuck me. Of course.

"Rats are so much smarter than people seem to realize," says Mark. Now he's selling me on rats. Right. "They're actually quite clever, they really are!"

I guess Mark had never heard of Rat-Bite Fever. Rats will defend themselves to the death, just like any cornered Point person would. When our neighbour's daughter Patricia, the one with the lazy eye, got bitten during the night years ago when we were all still little, she was never the same. First, she had all that pus that smelt so bad around the teeth marks on her leg, then a purple rash a few days later. She had a fever and chills for a couple of days, followed by vomiting and diarrhea for another few days after that. My mom told Patricia's mom that she had to take her to the hospital but she wouldn't listen, insisting the hospital would just call the welfare office and they'd be out on the streets again.

"Uh, don't they bite?" I asked Mark.

No need to let on that I knew all about the dangers of fucking rats. The idea that they had them in the basement of the school living in cages with three square meals a day made me want to start looking around for a blowtorch or Molotov cocktail.

"I mean, what do you do so they won't, you know, attack people working on them in the lab? So they won't bite?"

Mark gave me a patient smile.

"These are lab rats, of course, not wild rats. They're domestic, bred for the lab so they're much calmer and smaller and not aggressive at all compared to wild rats. Domestic rats can tolerate all kinds of conditions a wild rat wouldn't, of course. They can live with greater crowding and breed more easily and also produce more offspring."

Domestic rats? That sounds like they train them to clean rich people's homes. I listened as he talked about how the rate of learning could be measured by rats placed in a maze, showing them how to follow their way out through the use of food treats and then, after removing the cookie-crumb trails, leaving it up to them to figure it out on their own using logic, and seeing how quickly they learned the escape route. By the time he finished explaining it, I was starting to think rats are maybe going to one day rule the fucking world. But also, what kind of a sick mind creates a damn maze to stick a bunch of rats in? And just because a rat can learn something, how does that mean anything about how humans learn? Or is Mark secretly an even more dark person than I am? Thinking that most people are just like fucking rats?

"If you're interested in taking one home for a pet at the end of term, just let me know," said Mark. "We have to get rid of them anyway, and I'm sure one would prefer to go and live with you than to be exterminated in the lab. We're usually able to find homes for half of them."

I'm such an asshole. I actually had thought for a minute there that he really was flirting with me. But he's just looking for some foster homes for his freaky lab rats. Thank god he couldn't read my mind. I would have died of embarrassment. Mark looked at his watch and we both realized that the classroom had filled up behind us. Time to start class. Just as I was about to move towards my seat, Mark took a step closer and spoke softly.

"If you ever want to catch a coffee or a drink sometime after class, just let me know. I can tell you all about how to care for your rat and even let you take your pick of the litter."

Holy shit.

I didn't hear most of what Mark talked about in that class. I was too busy thinking about what having a drink with him would actually mean. I remembered suddenly, too, how one time he had casually mentioned when we were alone that it was a pleasure to have an older student like me in the class.

"Usually the students are all barely out of their teens. It's nice to have someone more… mature."

At the time I had thought the fucker was calling me old or something just because I was a bit older than the average student, since I had been out of high school for a couple of years before going back. Come to think of it, I wonder how old Mark is? He said something one time about being a psychologist. Doesn't that mean he's at least in his early thirties? Ugh, he's old.

Later in the school basement, I'm shocked by how cute the rats are. I'm shocked. Plenty of cute mice, too. They rush right up to the cage wall and wait to be petted through the wires. The rats look clean and even adorable. Mind you, these ones don't look like Point rats. These ones are practically Disney rats. Their fur is clean and shiny and soft to the touch. Their claws look tiny and their teeth are tucked inside their mouths and you only see them when they take one of their tiny pellets in both hands and eat it like a miniature cob of corn. They all have names like they're from Westmount: Oliver, Thomas and Carter. Charlotte, Chloe and Grace. These rats look friendly and happy. They're so curious about everything. Several are standing up on their back paws, their eyes following me around the room. Like puppies in a pet store, each one seems to be silently screaming, "Pick me! Pick me!"

"I can already tell which one you like," says Mark, smiling at me.

I admit, for an old guy, he's kind of gorgeous. Of course, he's wrong about me already knowing which one I want. But I know to play along.

"Which one do I want?" I smile back.

"You want them all," laughs Mark, and I admit I'm impressed as that's exactly what I had been thinking. I want every single one of them. The mice, too. They're playing with each other and only stopping every minute or so to take another peek at me and see what I'm doing.

"What happens to the ones that no one takes?"

"They have to be disposed of. They can't stay here over the summer, of course," says Mark.

I hate myself later for not asking why not. Why can't they stay in the lab for the summer? In their cages—their homes—playing with each other and being all curious and nosy about everything going on around them?

Later, when Jack walks into our apartment and sees the glass aquarium on the coffee table in the living room, he stops in his tracks.

"What in hell is that?"

"His name is Robbie," I say. "Isn't he beautiful?"

And he really is. Apparently, Robbie is a hooded rat, which means his body is a beautiful bright white with a glossy black hood covering his face. He's super friendly and eager to learn. He loves when I hold him and likes to snuggle close to my face. His tail is long and surprisingly thick. And his smell is clean, like the wood chips he sleeps on in his aquarium.

"You brought a rat into our apartment without even discussing it with me first? A pet?"

"I wanted to get your opinion on all of this, of course, but I had to make a quick decision. He's a lab rat from Dawson and if I hadn't taken him he would have been killed later today. I had no choice."

"No choice?" says Jack. His tone suggests I've just said something remarkably stupid. "There's always a choice. And of course he's a rat from Dawson. I didn't think you'd caught him in our yard."

"Do you want to hold him?" I know if Jack would only hold him he'd fall in love with him as much as I have. His sweet pink ears are so adorable and he's watching Jack as he paces around the room. Why can't he just look at him for a second? He'd instantly see how cute Robbie truly is.

"You know what? If a rat makes you happy, fine. I don't care. I gotta go. See you later."

Jack leaves before I can even ask him where's he's going.

I realize that I'm actually disappointed. A part of me had been all ready for the major blowout I knew would be coming. I had all of my arguments and ultimatums lined up and ready to pitch for the fight. Jack had rolled over way too easily. I'm nervous. I decide to call Annie.

"I can't tell you what to do," she says. "But you know already what you want so instead, let's talk about how you can get there. How you can get what you want."

I want to tell Annie that I've learned that everything I thought was true, everything I used believe, is a big fat lie. That I've put all my power into another person and I'm the biggest fool who is learning that payback really is a bitch. A fucking bitch. I'm still just two tiny baby steps away from the Point. I've finally learned that she was right all along. If I count on other people, something I never allowed myself to do before,

I'm only as strong or as weak as they are. But now I know what I want. I want Annie to quit the army. I want Annie to come home. I want Jack to love me like he did in the beginning. When he'd ask me what I was thinking and then listen to me when I told him. I want to stop bleeding like a stuck pig and be able to wear tampons again like a normal girl and not have to wear those thick pads that make me feel like I'm walking funny and everyone who sees me can tell what I did. I want Jack to ask me about the abortion. To tell me he's sorry and sad that I did what I did. Or he's angry and now hates me. I want Jack to talk to me. He can't pretend he doesn't know, either. When I pushed him away the other night, saying I was still bleeding and had to wait six weeks he didn't say a word, just rolled over to his side of the bed.

"I'm thinking of leaving," says Annie.

What? It takes a second for my brain to catch up with my ears before I can actually believe that I did in fact hear what Annie just said.

"Leaving? Leaving what?"

Leaving Halifax? Leaving the army?

"Leaving here. Coming back home."

For a second I'm frozen in place. I'm so thrilled that I don't trust that I've really heard what I think I just heard. It's my mind playing tricks on me again. It's been doing that for a while now, making me wake up sometimes and for a second think I'm still pregnant and that when I tell Jack he's going to pull me in for a hug and whisper into my hair that he can't believe he's having a baby with me and what will we call it if it's a boy? Or a girl?

"What do you think?" says Annie into the phone. "I thought you'd be happy…"

My screaming and jumping up and down meant I missed the rest of her sentence. Annie is coming home? For real?

"Don't mess with me!" I shriek into the phone. "Holy shit, for real?"

It takes me a second to realize Annie is crying. But it doesn't sound like happy tears at all.

"Are you okay?" I ask. "What is it, Annie? What is it?? Tell me!"

At first, I'm not sure what she's saying. But between her sobs she tells me that she can't do it anymore and has put in for an honourable discharge. Annie scored the highest in her platoon at graduation after basic training. I thought she loved the army.

"What happened?" I ask. I know now that something is terribly wrong. Annie wants to quit the army? No fucking way.

"I can't talk about it like this," she says. "I can't let anyone here hear me like this."

I realize that it doesn't even sound like Annie's voice now on the phone. I know people will say that someone sounds "broken," but seriously, that's exactly how Annie sounds. I've heard her when she's been and sounds exhausted. I've heard her when she's sounded scared, angry and frustrated, and we've plotted together many times during those kinds of periods. But this broken Annie is a new one. She's never sounded this kind of broken before.

"Come home," I say, and Annie sobs into the phone.

"You think so? You really think so? It's okay?" I hear her rapidly sniffing, and I can imagine her rubbing at her face trying to hide the tears from those assholes on the base.

"Absolutely. One hundred percent, for sure. Come home."

After I hang up the phone I look over at Robbie. His adorable little face is pressed up against the glass and he's looking at me. Who knew a rat could be so cute? So lovable? I lift him out of the aquarium and start to rub his back along his spine just the way he loves it. That's when I felt the lump. And then another lump. At first I thought it was my imagination, my mind just playing tricks on me. But later, much later, I'd always look back at this exact moment as the one just before my whole life went to shit.

"Do you feel it? Right there?"

It's later that night and I'm trying to get Jack to touch the right spot. I hate that I had to talk him into even trying. Even beg.

"Please, please just check it out. I think he has some weird lumps or something."

Jack doesn't want to have anything to do with Robbie. Although he'd laugh if I said this to his face, I know he hates him. He never did bond with him like I did. He never talks to him and refuses to hold him no matter how many times I've tried to get him to.

"It's a rat, for god's sake," he said when I finally openly complained that he never holds him. Never even looks at him.

"Hmmm, I do feel something here, and here," says Jack. He's touching the right spots now.

"What do you think? What do I do What does this mean?"

Jack looks at me and says slowly, "Nothing, I guess. I mean, what can you do? He's a rat. Uh, it's a 'he,' right?"

I don't know why Jack wants to pretend like he doesn't know that Robbie is a boy. Why he wants to hurt me like this.

"Just give him to me," I say and reach for him.

After dropping Robbie back down into his soft bedding, as I gently drag the cover over the top of the aquarium, I hear the front door shut. Jack has left without saying goodbye. Again. I don't know what made me do it but I suddenly decided to go through all of Jack's stuff. I feel embarrassed even as I'm doing it. I know it's wrong. I don't even know what I'm looking for. What I expect or hope to find. Proof. Proof of what? And then I find it. Tucked into his sock drawer inside of one of his socks I feel something hidden away in the toe. I pull it out, a small bulge, and I'm holding four packages of condoms all tightly pressed together. Trojan. There's actually a name on the packages. Trojan. I hold one up close to my face and I'm surprised to see some printing on it. I guess I've never actually seen a condom still in its wrapper before. The writing reads to me like broken English. It's in bold script:

"Best condoms. Trojan Charged orgasmic pleasure condoms."

I wonder if they all have writing on them? Are there lots of different brands? What makes a guy pick one package of condoms over another? I wonder if the brand name Trojan is playing off the story "The Trojan Horse." So the sperm hidden or tucked inside the tip of the condom are... what exactly? The invaders? Is someone messing with men by selling them condoms like this? Or do men just grab the ones closest to the edge of the shelf and rush to the cash with it. I somehow can't imagine anyone, least of all a guy, standing there and actually reading the labels and trying to decide which ones sounds "best." Hell, shouldn't the packages be bragging about the condoms being break-proof instead of, like this one, being "ultra-thin"? Or coated with something that, should a couple of sperm make it through somehow, they'll be blasted to hell by some kind of a spermicide? I know I'm keeping my mind busy from thinking about the obvious but eventually it goes there and I can't deny the question any further. Why in hell does Jack have condoms when he knows I'm on the pill? And have been for quite some time now? Whose vagina is getting Trojan Charged orgasmic pleasure with my Jack? I hear the sound of Robbie moving in the next room as he hits the top of his aquarium with his head. He does that sometimes as if to remind me that he's there. Waiting. Needing me.

"I think Robbie has cancer," says Mark in the morning.

I had taken Robbie with me to the school the next day, hoping Mark could tell me what is wrong.

"These look and feel like tumours." Mark doesn't hesitate to gently probe and rub his fingers along Robbie's spine, rubbing behind his ears and then going back to the lumpy spots. I'm trying to give myself a second to absorb the idea that Robbie has cancer, cancer tumours, by focusing on how Mark hasn't forgotten Robbie's name. Mark also knows Robbie is a boy.

"Are you sure?" It's the only think I can think of to say.

"Oh, for sure," says Mark. "It's how most of them eventually die."

"Most of them?"

"The lab rats," says Mark. "Of course, cancer is fairly common among all rats, but lab rats in particular are especially vulnerable."

"They… are?"

"Yeah, some think it's because of the genetically modified corn they're fed that they develop all the tumours but there's also a lot of evidence that suggests that lab rats were already prone to developing cancer even before GMOs showed up."

I'm wondering, how did I end up with a pet that was apparently already doomed to die of cancer before I even knew it was a problem. Why did I pick this to love?

"So even sewer rats get cancer? Tumours?"

I already know now that Mark is going to say yes and it kind of makes sense in a way. I mean these furry fuckers are running around in filthy sewers, inhaling lead and shit and corruption all day. If it's not the wide end of a baseball bat, sharp edge of a heavy boot, or the short end of a .45, what else are they gonna die from, right?

"Yes, wild rats commonly die from cancer," says Mark, "the ones who live long enough to manage to escape predators. And the lab ones are bred to be so similar genetically, it means they're even more predisposed to the same genetic susceptibilities. Like cancer. I'm sorry. Maybe I should have warned you?"

Yeah. Maybe he should have.

"I guess I just didn't think about how long Robbie might live or what he might ever die of…"

"If it makes you feel any better," says Mark, "none of them live for very long, anyway. Two or maybe three years, tops."

Why does he think that might make me feel any better?

"I've had Robbie for much less than even one year!"

"Yeah, I understand how unfair it must feel to you," says Mark. He's standing closer now and reaches over and rubs the top of my right shoulder.

"You're welcome to pick another one, hell, even two if you want them, at the end of this term. I'll even give you pick of the litter!"

Is every man on the planet a fucking idiot?

"So, what do I do about Robbie, though? Like, is there any treatment or anything I could do."

Mark is holding up his hand.

"No, no, no. Sorry, there's nothing you can do but maybe help him along the way so he isn't uncomfortable or unhappy or in any kind of pain. You could leave him here right now if you want. I could take care of it for you."

Does he mean he'll kill Robbie for me?

"We use carbon dioxide. He'll just go to sleep. No pain. Easy. I promise."

Later, when I get home with Robbie, I decide he should have a cage instead of an aquarium. He's a rat. Not a damn fish.

156

Chapter Eleven

NANNY SAYS THE QUEEN ALWAYS sticks her pinky finger out stiff and straight like a pencil whenever she's holding a teacup, glass of water, or any kind of cup or glass for anything.

"It's the Royal way," says Nanny.

I started copying Nanny as a kid, always holding that pinky out whenever I'd drink anything and now it's such a habit I can't remember not to do it.

"You look like an idiot," says Ruth.

Apparently it's a look only Nanny and the Queen can pull off. But of course I'm never going to admit to Ruth that I don't do it on purpose. At least not anymore. When I was a kid I thought it was pretty cool and practiced doing it for weeks and weeks until I was able to do it without even thinking about it. I figured someone somewhere somehow was going to notice me doing it and think I might be related to the Royal Family. Pretty cool, right? Yeah, I know. Ruth is right. It makes me look like an idiot. Now I just need to unlearn how to do it.

"That's a perfect example of classical conditioning," says Jack. "You've paired the belief that someone will assume you're royalty with the stiff finger sticking out every time you pick up any drinking vessel. It's going to be tough to break yourself of the habit."

He's laughing so hard while he says this I'm surprised the shit head can even form a complete sentence. I didn't know he had been listening to me whine about it on the phone to Annie, telling her I was still doing it sometimes without thinking and it's getting embarrassing now. Hell, I didn't even think we were talking anymore.

"So are you seriously thinking of moving?" asks Jack once he's finished laughing.

I realize he's overheard the entire conversation. Not just the stiff baby finger part.

"Well, it looks increasingly impossible for me to stay here, right?"

Oh god, please let him jump up and tell me I'm acting crazy. That he loves me. That he's not letting me go anywhere, no way. I have to stay right here. With him.

"Yes, but it doesn't mean you have to move all the way to Hamilton, right? What about school? Your job?"

What about us?

"I only have another semester with Dawson, anyway. And McMaster, a real university, has offered me a spot in the Arts program. I'm sure I can get another job. Out there."

Most of that is bullshit I've just made up on the spot. I'm curious now to see how far Jack is willing to go with the idea of me just moving, and moving so far away. To the armpit of Canada. Jack has been mocking the city of Hamilton since the day my family left.

"It's ironic they think that by moving to Hamilton they're somehow escaping their poverty roots. Poverty isn't defined just by location. It shapes your behaviours, attitudes and continues to follow you throughout the rest of your life. White trash is white trash even when it moves in with the good stuff."

Jesus. I had called him a jerk and hit him with the pillow from our bed after he said all that, yelling at him for calling my family white trash.

"It's okay, it's okay," laughed Jack as he tried to pin me down. "I actually like white trash."

Why did that seem so funny then? Why does it make my blood boil now?

"Hmmmm," says Jack. "You probably could get a job in the sociology department at McMaster. Just ask, what's his name? Mark? Yeah, just ask Mark to write you a letter. I'm sure they could use more hands in the labs."

Then he leans over and picks his textbook back up and opens it, making it clear that our conversation is now over. I want to set his book on fire. I want to set him on fire. How did I become invisible? When did that happen?

"So are we… done?"

Jack looks up and puts on a fake look of surprise.

"Done? Are we… done? Are you pretending to have just figured that out now?"

I know I have choices to make now. But I don't like any of them. I decide to take the phone in the bathroom and call Annie again.

"How soon do you think you'll be back here?"

Then I remember that for her, coming back home doesn't mean Montreal. It means living wherever Mom and Dad are. Mom has a job in an underground parking lot now in Hamilton. It's for the largest mall in the city, Jackson Square. Mom validates the tickets and collects the cash payments after shoppers retrieve their vehicles and have to pass by her small booth to get the yellow arm lifted to let them out of the parking lot. Mom amuses herself by saying dumb stuff to them as she hands them back their ticket stub, knowing they won't believe their own ears when she says, "Fuck you very much!" At Christmastime some of the drivers would actually give her a small tip with their payment and Mom would smile and say, "Merry Kiss My Ass!" as they pulled away.

"It's always funny to see the confused look on their faces," says Mom.

Apparently, every single driver gives her the benefit of the doubt, certain they've misunderstood or misheard what she said as the thought of an underground parking lot attendant saying anything outright rude to them is unthinkable. Who would have the nerve, right? So she never gets complained about. Not even once.

"I love my job," says Mom.

I'm still shocked Mom actually quit the clinic. She was making more money there than all of the nurses and doctors since they pay according to how many dependents you have, the idea being it's only fair on account of Mom having six kids that she should be paid more than someone with fewer or no kids. None of the doctors or nurses has six kids. Dad says it's the only time he thinks the commies got it right. I made a dumb joke one time about how maybe Mom should have had more kids and no one laughed. But still, she quit? The clinic? I thought it was her favourite child.

"Mom was tired of fighting battles she knew she was never going to win," explained Ruth one time after I kept going on about being shocked that Mom had been willing to leave that hefty paycheque behind.

"And don't forget her nervous breakdown," added Ruth.

Funny, I always do forget about Mom's nervous breakdown. The whole concept seems so weird to me. I mean, what is a nervous breakdown exactly, anyway? Of course, I know better than to ever say out loud, especially to any of my sisters, that I always thought that was just Mom being her usual attention-seeking drama-queen self. Mom can't just ask for help outright like a regular person. You know, admit that she's still hurting over the way she grew up and all the shit she had to deal with. And a useless mother. If it wasn't her father hurting her, or her useless mother saying, "Come away from the girls, Alfred," then it was the hunger or the humiliation of having to go to school with dirty hair and fingernails from trying to help catch the filthy rats, dusty with lead from the narrow sewer pipes. No. Mom was never going to ask for help for that. She had to pick something less shameful, of course. Something that made her the hero instead of the gross little girl no one even loved enough to feed, never mind protect from the cold, the rats, or the men and boys in her household. So yeah, I always do forget about Mom's nervous breakdown. I always thought she should have just said she was done with trying to save a world that didn't know how or maybe didn't even want to be saved. Done with giving away half her paycheque and still not making any real dent.

"Your father got a job at the bank at Jackson Square!" says Mom into the phone. "He started yesterday. They wanted him so bad they would have had him start right after the interview! I swear he was hired just because of how handsome he looked in his suit."

My dad is working at a bank?

"What does he... do?"

"Well, you know your father," says Mom. "He'll be practically running the damn place before he's done."

I want to ask for more details but it feels rude somehow to push.

"Him and your sister are going to look at renting some horses this weekend, after he gets off," says Mom.

I know which sister that is. And I know Mom is super proud and even showing off a little by saying Dad is going to be renting a horse. Horses are the pets of rich people. They don't take lab rats home. But what do you actually do with a *rented* horse, anyway?

Not too long after moving to the armpit of Canada, all of my sisters had their lives all straightened out. Beth is working at Olive Garden, a restaurant at the mall. She'd been working at a 7/11 until one night two guys came in to rob the place and Beth had a knife held to her throat by the smaller one while the taller one emptied out the cash. When the dumb Hamilton *Spectator* ran an article the next day they included Beth's name in the story. She knew never to go back to the store after that and found herself a new job at Olive Garden just a few days later.

"People are so gross," says Beth. "They actually eat octopus at my place. Honestly, for real."

I ask how they store them at the restaurant and wonder if they have them in a large tank, like some places do with lobsters so the rich people coming in can play God and tell them which one to kill and cook up for them.

"No," says Beth. "They're already dead and chopped up into pieces and dipped in a batter and then deep-fried."

I admit I kind of want to try one now. Or at least a tiny bite. Deep-fried, right?

"But they're sneaky," says Beth. "They don't call it 'octopus' of course. On the menu they call it 'calamari.' Which apparently is code for octopus."

Beth and I agree that people can be so gross about what they consider worth eating. I mean, it's not like I eat the best stuff all the time, either, of course. But to go into a place and pay money to eat something prehistoric, like an octopus? That's just sick, right?

"I'm going to have enough saved up soon to quit, though," says Beth.

She's hoping to save up enough to go to nursing school, of course. Everybody still wants to be Annie.

"I got a job at a weight-loss clinic," says Annie.

"As soon as I can get into the General Hospital, though, I'm out of here," says Annie. She's been trying to get a job at the General for months but they just aren't hiring nurses right now.

"But hey, it pays the bills, right?"

A weight-loss what?

"Seriously. People actually pay money to come in and get weighed each week, tell me about what they've been eating so I can judge them, go over their exercise and food plan with me so I can tell them where they went wrong, then buy some of the super-expensive special food the place sells to help you lose weight."

I don't even know where to begin. Annie is always doing something so fucking interesting. The army and now this. Rich people paying money to get beat up.

"So what's so special about it? The food?"

I always thought you lost weight by eating less, not by eating any kind of special or magical food.

"It's not their main food, of course," explains Annie. "The diet they follow is super healthy, with lots of vegetables and salads and high-quality protein. The special foods they can buy from us are like low-calorie treats. Like teeny chocolate chip cookies and small bags of baked, not deep-fried, chips. It's all about portion control. The cookies are so tiny they can have eight of them and feel like, you know, they got to pig out when they really haven't."

Who knew Annie could be such a salesperson? I want to join the clinic myself now. Not to lose weight but to get some of those healthy foods she's talking about.

"What's a 'high-quality' protein?" I ask.

I've got a million jokes to make and I need Annie to give me my opening for the perfect joke.

"Well, lean chicken, most fish…"

Jesus. No jokes about sperm or quick loads today, I guess. Annie is really into her new job.

"Uh, so I guess you love it, right?"

"Hell no!" says Annie. "I hate it, of course. They even make me wear a white uniform. To make it seem more professional and medical."

I don't understand. If she's telling people what to eat or not to eat to make them skinny, isn't that kind of medical? Isn't that what real doctors do? Tell you that you need to gain or lose some weight? Tell you where you're fucking up and tell you what to do instead?

"These are pretty unhappy women," says Annie. "They hate their bodies so much it would shock you. They all think they're fat and most of them really aren't. I think they come just to punish themselves to be honest."

"To punish themselves? For what exactly?"

Man, rich women are so fucking weird.

"I don't know why they hate themselves or what they're trying to punish themselves for," says Annie, "maybe they don't even know. But it's pretty horrible. Sometimes they even cry as they talk about losing control that week and eating stuff they wish they hadn't. For going off their food plans. I can always tell who cheated and who didn't just from the way they walk into my office. I wish I could afford to quit."

Annie has an office? Damn. She laughs when I say into the phone, "Yawn. Rich people's problems."

Ruth is working at a video game repair shop if you can believe it. She does the books, cleans up the place and does most of the talking to the customers. Apparently the shop owner is a genius when it comes to fixing machines but he's terrible with people.

"I just get them to explain it all to me, like a middle man," says Ruth, "then I explain it to him. It works better this way."

Although she despises her job I know Ruth has started liking some guy named Larry. She isn't officially dating him yet or anything, just secretly mooning over him whenever he comes into her work. He kind of looks like the actor Kevin Bacon.

"I just like talking to him," says Ruth, but her face goes red and she looks away when she says that. Yup, she's got it bad. I saw her face one time when Larry showed up and I never saw her look more happy, and as weird as this sounds, awake. If she had a tail, I bet it'd wag every time she sees this Larry guy. I hope he's not a jerk. I hope he likes her half as much as I can tell she likes him. Like Beth, Ruth is saving up until she can go to nursing school, too. She figures she'll have enough in about a year and until then, when she's not at work she's at home studying from Annie's old nursing school books. She even has most of Annie's old notebooks and is always saying thank god Annie has such neat handwriting. Our sister Julia is in Ottawa working at a jewellery store. My sisters told me they think she's in love with the guy at the store who went to Ottawa U to learn all about fancy stones and stuff and now cuts the diamonds for the store. His job sounds boring as hell, but apparently he's hot as hell. So it's not the diamond cutting that's keeping Julia close to Ottawa for the moment.

I'm glad to learn that Hanna has finally registered at one of the local high schools. Mom kept putting her off every time Hanna asked for her help to get into the school system, saying maybe she should just get a job.

"But I don't want to be a high school dropout," explained Hanna who, you guessed it, also wants to be a damn nurse and knows she can't become one without first graduating from high school. See? Everyone really does want to be exactly like Annie. And why wouldn't they? After Hanna cried to Annie, saying she didn't know what she was going to do about getting back into school, Annie took the morning off work and brought her to the school herself. Hanna started the very next day. So all my sisters have their lives all worked out. And here I am, the fuck-up once again. About to lose my boyfriend, become homeless and quit my job and leave school. Again.

"Why don't you just move out here and live with me in Hamilton for a while?" says Annie. "You know, until you have it all figured out. I mean, why not go to McMaster? Admit it. You love school. Why would you not go?"

Fuck me. I want to be a nurse now, too. But me and Jack might still have a shot.

I need to think about my choices and just make a decision.

They had told me not to take any baths for a while after the abortion procedure, warning me it could make me bleed. I wondered if they meant it could make a person bleed to death but I knew they'd think I was being weird if I asked so I didn't. I wonder if that girl who cried herself to death was really the girl who bled herself to death but Nanny will never say that and added the tears instead? I mean, no matter how many times I roll it around in my head it just doesn't make sense. You can't cry yourself to death. No matter what. But you can bleed, right?

"You can go now," the nurse had said. I keep thinking about that day, even all these weeks later. I had been sitting in a huge chair for about half an hour or so, in a special waiting area just for the baby killers. At first I froze, not sure what to do next. It's like I had forgotten how to stand up, how to do whatever it is a person is supposed to do next.

"Are you okay?" asks the nurse. I know she's worried I'm about to make her day harder. This isn't the Diana nurse, dropping "sweeties" left and right, rubbing your arm and offering tight hugs.

"No, no, I'm fine," I smile at her. "Just waiting for... a second."

Saying I'm waiting for "a second" sounds less fake than saying I'm waiting for courage. Later, when I got home, I watched reruns of *Little House on the Prairie* for a few days. How come I never realized before how great this show is? I'm crying as the dad cries and hugs his girls. The mom is so pretty with her hair in one long braid that she wraps around her head. When Jack suddenly walks in and catches me watching it I feel so embarrassed I blurt out that it's part of an assignment for school.

"You know, I have to write something about it for my sociology class."

Jack thinks TV makes people dumber and had reluctantly agreed to us even having a TV in the first place and only after I'd insisted, saying it wouldn't look like a real living room to me without a TV in it.

"Why are you crying?" he asks with a mean laugh. "Isn't that... what? *Little House on the Prairie*?"

Yeah, I know I'm a complete lame ass. But come on, how can you watch as this sweet family with the simplest of shit go through all kinds of hardships and dramas week after week yet still supporting each other through it all and *not* cry, right? I mean, when Mary went blind? I mean, totally fucking BLIND? The rest of us would have just given up, right? Sure, they had her all angry and upset for a few episodes but when she finally turned around and found herself again? Holy shit, right? Jack's a fucking snob.

"Didn't you watch any TV at all as a kid, growing up?"

I can tell he's trying to decide whether to be honest.

"Sure, when my parents were in control of my leisure time as a child I was like anyone else, I guess, and watched some stuff, sure. How else would I know what's part of popular culture right now?"

Part of popular culture? Who fucking even talks like that?

"So what did you watch?" I admit I'm dying to know. Or at least curious as to what he's going to claim he watched.

"Well, I don't know. I guess I watched what everybody was watching back then. *The Flintstones*, *The Jetsons*, *The Bugs Bunny Show*, all of the popular-at-the-time kiddy crap."

What a major lame ass. Why am I so thrilled that I got Jack to admit he watched *The* fucking *Flintstones*? *The Flintstones*! Jack senses my superior attitude somehow.

"So what did *you* watch?" he demands. I know to slowly smile and look like I need to think it over. To remember.

"Well, it must have been a little good, right? You know, for you to remember what all of those shows were called, right?"

"Oh stop it! You can't make me feel bad for being subjected to the cultural norms of my time!"

How come I never noticed before that Jack so obviously lacks a sense of humour?

"And why would your class make you have to watch reruns of one of the dumbest shows ever on TV, anyway?"

It somehow suddenly feels like my job now to defend the honour of *Little House on the Prairie.*

"It's not 'dumb.' You could argue it's even historical!" I admit it was weird watching a western that didn't seem to include any Indians, ever.

Jack snorts so loudly I want to punch him in his balls.

"Historical?" he sneers. "Really? Is that the best you can do?"

I realize it was a smart move not to tell Jack what I'm really growing in the bathroom after all, though I still wish I could ask him why the hell did he think I keep the lights on in there 24/7. Annie had urged me not to tell him but it had felt wrong, like I was keeping a secret from him.

"Well, it is a secret," said Annie, "but it's an important one. People like Jack won't understand and might, you know, judge you or something."

I suddenly realize that Annie is maybe not such a huge fan of Jack after all.

"You think he's judgmental?"

"Maybe a little," said Annie carefully.

"But that's not such a terrible thing, of course. It just means he didn't get exposed to a lot of… well… you know… stuff. I mean, when he was growing up and all. But that's good, right?"

Annie and I have talked about the cluelessness people like Jack often show and have agreed we secretly, much to our shame, think it's kind of, well, somehow attractive in its own way. Like they still think the world is fair and if you work hard, know exactly what you want, then things will actually happen the way you want it to. Kind of like a cute but clueless child.

"It's not Jack's fault," says Annie, and I know she wants to just distract me from the fact that she let it slip a bit that she's maybe not the fan I had somehow been assuming she is.

I'm realizing just how true it is what Ruth said one time, about how life is learning where exactly your line in the sand is and then just choosing the lesser of two or three or ten evils.

I try to decide which is the lesser evil, but all of my options seem shitty. Like a rat having to choose between getting crushed under someone's boot, drowning in a toilet, or growing a bunch of tumours. So what the hell do I do? I wish I could talk to Jack. I wish I could ask him what he thinks about all of this. But I guess that would be kind of like trying to discuss all the highlights of a funeral with the person you just buried.

"What's the timeline here?" says Jack the next morning. I decide on the spot not to make it any easier for him from now on.

"Timeline?"

"Uh, yeah…"

I just look at him and wait. He looks away. I pick up my book bag and leave for school. Sitting on the metro I suddenly realize I forgot to kiss Robbie goodbye.

"I want you to think about how you might approach interviewing elites versus refugees. What would you do differently in each case, and why?"

My sociology professor is reading off our midterm exam questions. She always does that before she even lets us begin to write our answers.

"This way, if you have any questions you can just ask them right away and let everyone else hear the answers at the same time. If one of you is wondering about something, I guarantee you aren't alone."

Her exams and assignments are always interesting. I mean that first question right off the bat is such a good one, right? Forget what the answer might even be, I wish I could sit with Annie for a while and just yak away about the question itself. Before Dawson, I wouldn't have even thought to wonder about shit like that. I never even gave a thought to refugees before I came here. Maybe didn't even know what that was exactly, either.

"Distinguish between covert and semi-covert research. Under what circumstances might a researcher use deception in their projects?"

Whoa. This is a good example of what I mean about fancy education. Instead of saying words like "bullshit," or "lies," they say words like "deception," which sounds so much better, right?

"Where do stereotypes come from?"

Holy shit. See what I mean? I was the last one to leave the exam. I would have done almost anything to be able to read what the other students wrote. Before Dawson, I used to actually believe there are right and wrong answers to everything and used to just wish I knew what the right ones were. It sucks being wrong. And who doesn't want to be right? But Dawson is making me realize that it's not that simple. I could read every book in the world and learn everything there is to learn and still be wrong, or less right, about some shit.

"You have ten more minutes."

The prof is looking at me from the front of the room. She's being nice but I can sense her impatience for me to hurry the hell up and just hand my damn exam in. I'm trying to memorize all the questions, though. I want to talk about them with Annie. I know I can't just whip out a piece of paper and write them all down. I did that one time and got hauled into her office afterwards and was almost failed, even expelled.

"I saw you taking notes during the exam."

She's holding my "notes" in her hand. She had stood behind me for a few minutes while I was copying the answers down and I hadn't even realized she had snuck up behind me until she suddenly grabbed at my paper.

"Wait for me outside," she said softly. "Take your stuff and go into the hall."

I started to say I wasn't finished the exam yet but her face made it clear I had to go. Immediately. When she joined me in the hall later, after the class had cleared out, she told me to join her in her office. I followed behind her, my face bright red. I knew I had fucked up big time. Just wasn't sure yet how exactly.

"Why were you copying the exam and taking notes?" she got right into it the second we were both sitting. Her office is arranged so a student isn't sitting across from her desk. Instead, you're sitting right next to her since she has the desk on an angle. Dad would say she's a communist. Maybe even a dyke.

"Uh, I don't know." It's all I can think of to say.

She looks at me for a minute.

"Okay, let's start over. I know you're a good student. I can see you're always obviously paying close attention to the lectures. You don't speak often but when you do you demonstrate a clear understanding of the readings and are able to articulate your critical insights extremely well. So help me. Please. Help me to understand… this."

She thinks I'm giving some kind of "critical insights" in class? Wow. Oh wait. First they soften you up with a compliment, and then they blow up the ground underneath you. I remember how this works.

"It's nothing."

"Well, it is certainly something," she says. She leans over and taps the paper.

"This could be misconstrued to be a violation of the school's policy on cheating. One could assume you are making detailed notes of the exam so you can sell it to the students who were absent today and would now have an advanced look at the exam."

Jesus Christ. I guess there are scammers everywhere? Maybe it's the look on my face after what she just said but suddenly she seemed to decide to change tactics.

"Of course, I don't think that's what's happening here. I don't think you're dishonest. I don't think you are trying to cheat or do anything wrong. But I do want to understand it."

Uh, right. I would rather go to work and do a shift for free, or even have to listen to Nanny drone on for the millionth time about the Book of Revelation—the last book of the Bible—with its Four Horsemen of the Apocalypse and the Beast with his tattooed 666 buried in his hairline—rather than admit to copying her damn questions just so I could talk about them with my sister.

"Are you accusing me of something?"

I decide to go on the offense, something Dad taught me to do a long time ago. And it works.

"Oh my, of course not! I'm sorry. I really am. I just think you need to be aware, though, of how something… looks. And taking any kind of notes during an exam? About the exam? Well, you can appreciate, I'm sure, how that… well, how that… looks."

I know I have to pick my battles.

"I'm sorry if I broke any rules or policies. I won't do that again. I actually really enjoy your class and sometimes I like to think about the questions later. You know, like you said, there's no absolute "right" or "wrong" with some of these ideas and issues so I like to take a few quick notes to remind myself for later, the stuff I want to… revisit."

Dad would have been proud. At first I worried maybe I'd gone a little overboard but she lapped it up like a thirsty cat.

"Oh golly, oh my! Well that explains it perfectly!"

She literally clapped her hands. Even said the word "golly."

"You're making that part up," said Annie later, and she's right. I admit I can't help myself. Sometimes I need to add just the right detail, like the dumb word "golly," to make sure I'm getting it across just right. I need Annie to "get" just how fucking delighted this prof was by what I had said. And come on, saying she clapped her hands? Perfect, right? And she really did do that part. I think all stories need to be told that way. If you're trying to convey a certain sense or feeling about something, the "truth" sometimes just gets in the way. What matters, what really matters, is what's left behind. Afterwards. What does the whole truth get you?

Chapter Twelve

I GUESS ONE GOOD THING about having less to choose from is that you don't have as much to struggle and agonize over. With limited choices you just have to choose between Door A or Door B. Jack has taken away Doors C and D. I'd been thinking about leaving but suddenly the choice has been made for me, I'm the one being left.

"I'm assuming you don't want most of the furniture, except for the TV, right?"

That's one way to tell someone it's time to move out, right? I want to ask him why he doesn't want to still be roommates at least and keep splitting the rent.

"I can arrange the truck rental for you and get your stuff all loaded and delivered wherever you want. I've been looking in the paper and you could easily afford a place in the Point on your own. I figure you'd feel more comfortable back in familiar territory so I even called a few places for you if you want to have a look. There's one on Wellington Street that won't cost you much more than what your share of the rent here is. You could move in next week."

Next week is in three days. I'm barely making my share of the rent here now as it is and only because Jack has always paid for all the utilities and most, if not all, of our food. I want to tell him that even the worst slum landlord in the Point usually gave my mom a week's notice before kicking her ass out and hauling all of our stuff out on the sidewalk.

"They probably won't have any problem with your little pet over there, either," laughs Jack as he nods towards Robbie in his cage. "I mean they already have plenty of those living there already, anyway, right?"

He honesty thinks he's being funny.

"So what do you think?" He's giving me a huge smile. "Should I get the truck here for Monday? Or would Tuesday work better?"

I waited until later, after he had left. I looked over at Robbie's cage and realized he wasn't looking out through the bars like he usually does. I feel bad that I haven't been holding him as much lately. Ashamed to admit he even seems kind of gross to me now, lying there all bloated looking, his tumours slightly bulging and new ones popping up every day. His eyes seem less happy to see me now, too. I think he hates me. Maybe even blames me for his tumours. His cancer.

"Did you really mean it when you said I could move in with you?"

Without thinking about it too much I just picked up the phone when I got home from work that night and called Annie. Jack still wasn't back so I realized he was probably staying overnight with his French whore again and wouldn't be back until later next week, once he was sure I was gone.

"You can be honest," I said to Annie on the phone. "Did you mean it?"

Silence at the other end of the phone. I'm holding my breath now.

"Fucking right, I did!" shrieks Annie into the phone. "Don't play with me. For real? You gonna move down here to Hamilton with me?"

"Yeah," I say, smiling into the phone.

"I can fucking hardly wait."

I hear Robbie move behind me, walking across the cage, his little paws crunching on the wood chips.

He turns around and starts to chew on his own tail.

SELECTED NON-FICTION FROM VÉHICULE PRESS

With a Closed Fist: Growing Up in Canada's Toughest Neighbourhood
by Kathy Dobson

Canada's Forgotten Slaves: Two Hundred Years of Bondage
by Marcel Trudel, translated by George Tombs

*Wrestling with Colonialism on Steroids: Quebec Inuit
Fight for Their Homeland* by Zebedee Nungak

A Place in Mind: Designing Cities for the 21st Century
by Avi Friedman

The Art and Passion of Guido Nincheri
by Mélanie Grondin

A Stone in My Shoe: In Search of Neighbourhood
by George Ellenbogen

*Health Care and Politics: An Insider's View on Managing
and Sustaining Health Care in Canada*
by David Levine

Off the Books: A Jazz Life by Peter Leitch

Montreal of Yesterday: Jewish Life in Montreal 1900-1920
by Israel Medres, translated by Vivian Felsen

Rue Fabre: Centre of the Universe
by Jean-Claude Germain, translated by Donald Winkler

Of Jesuits and Bohemians: Tales of My Early Youth
by Jean-Claude Germain, translated by Donald Winkler

Véhicule Press